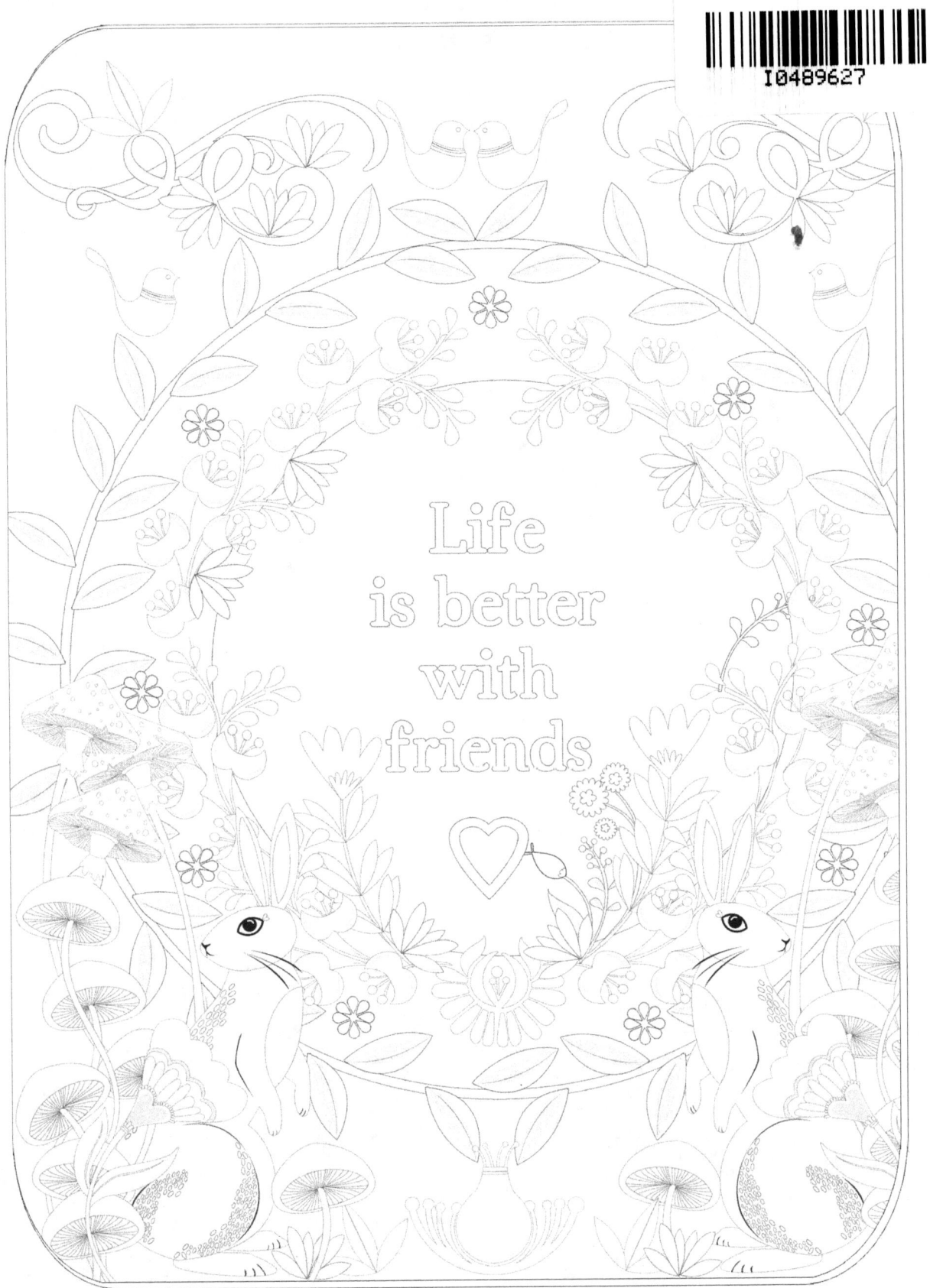

Life
is better
with
friends

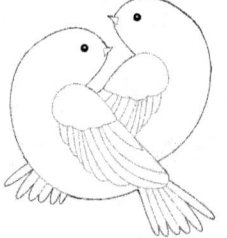

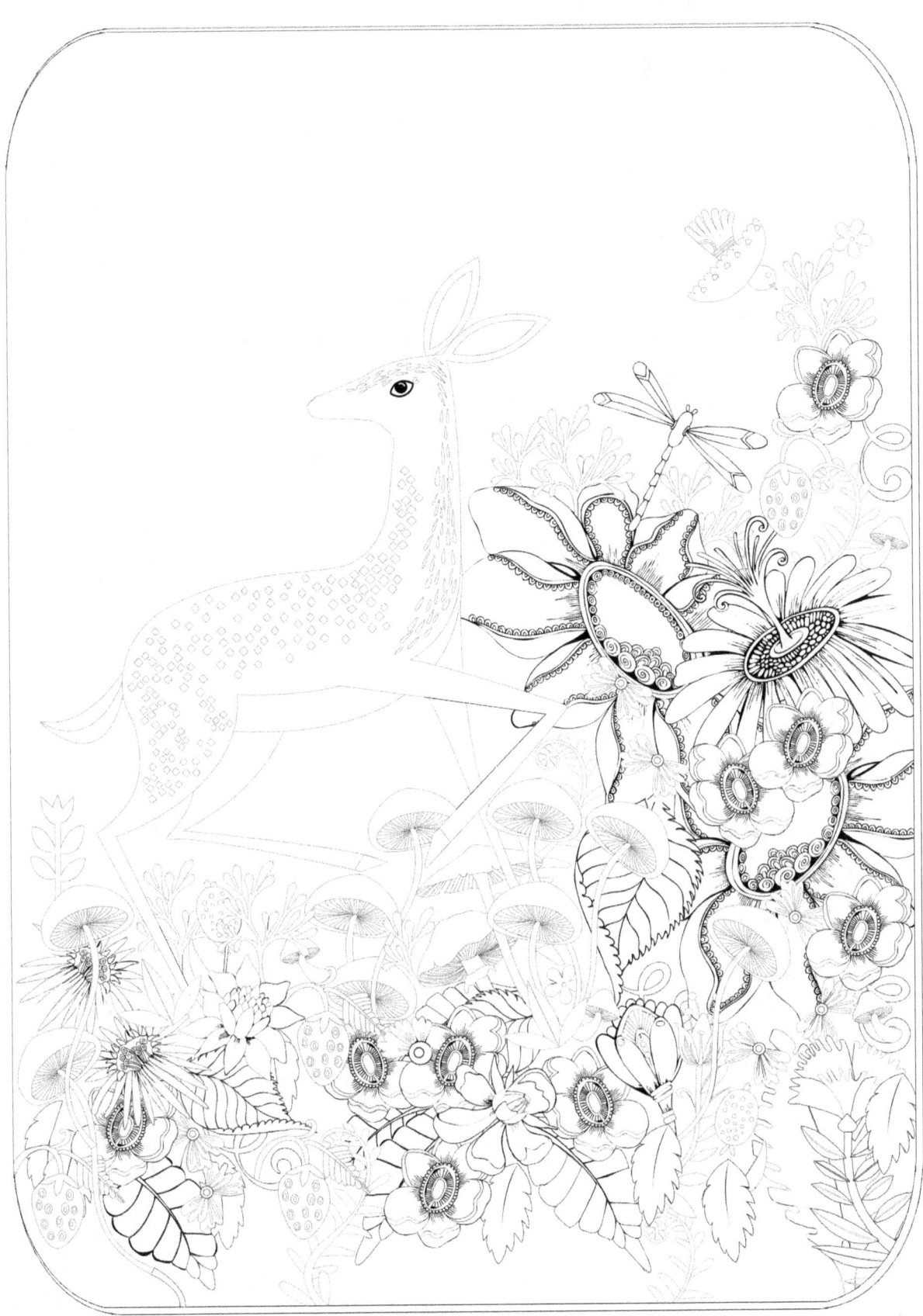

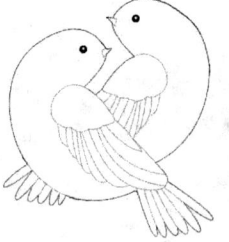

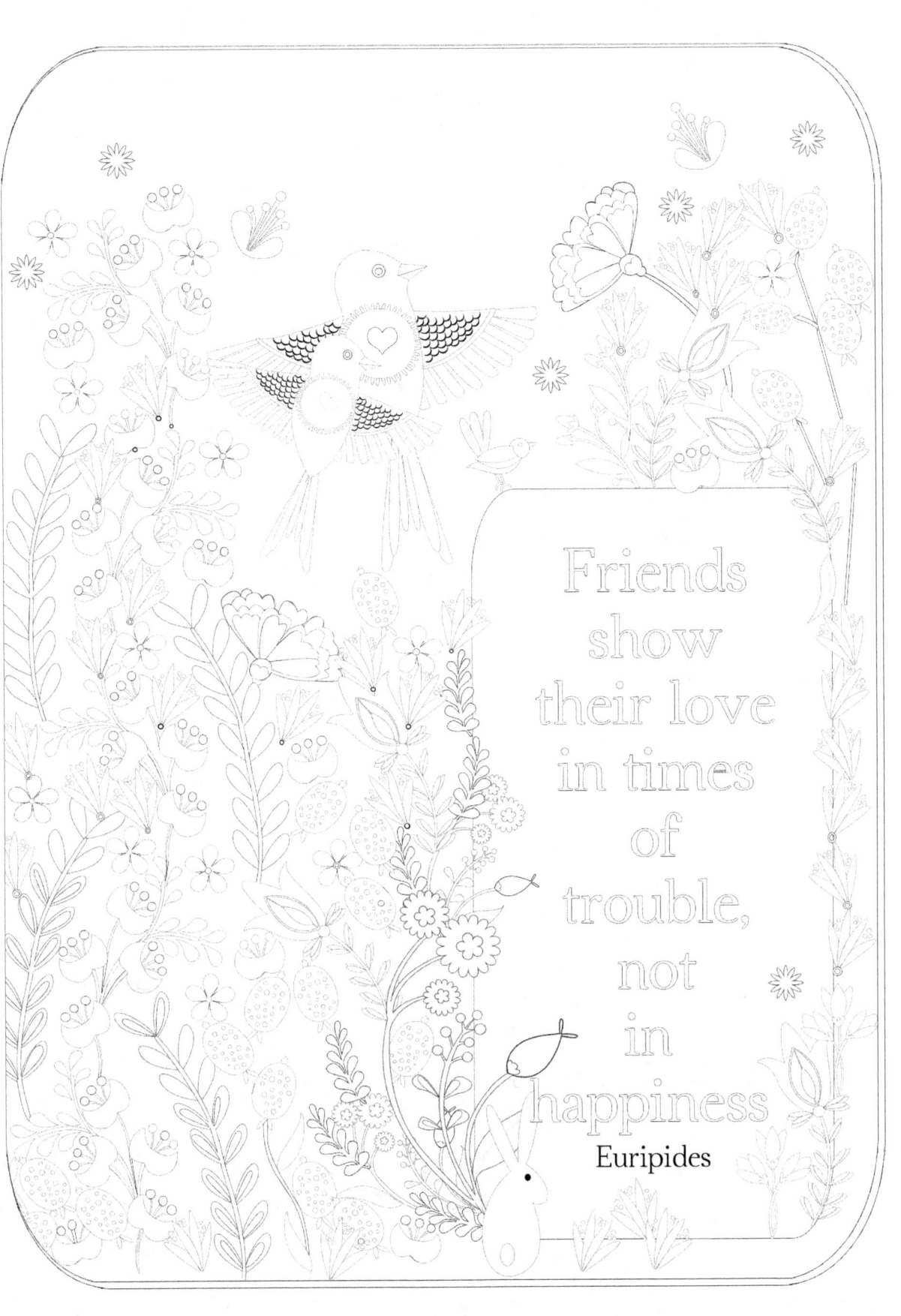

Friends
show
their love
in times
of
trouble,
not
in
happiness

Euripides

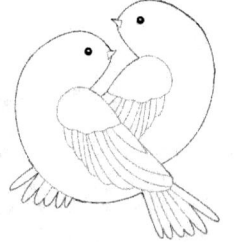

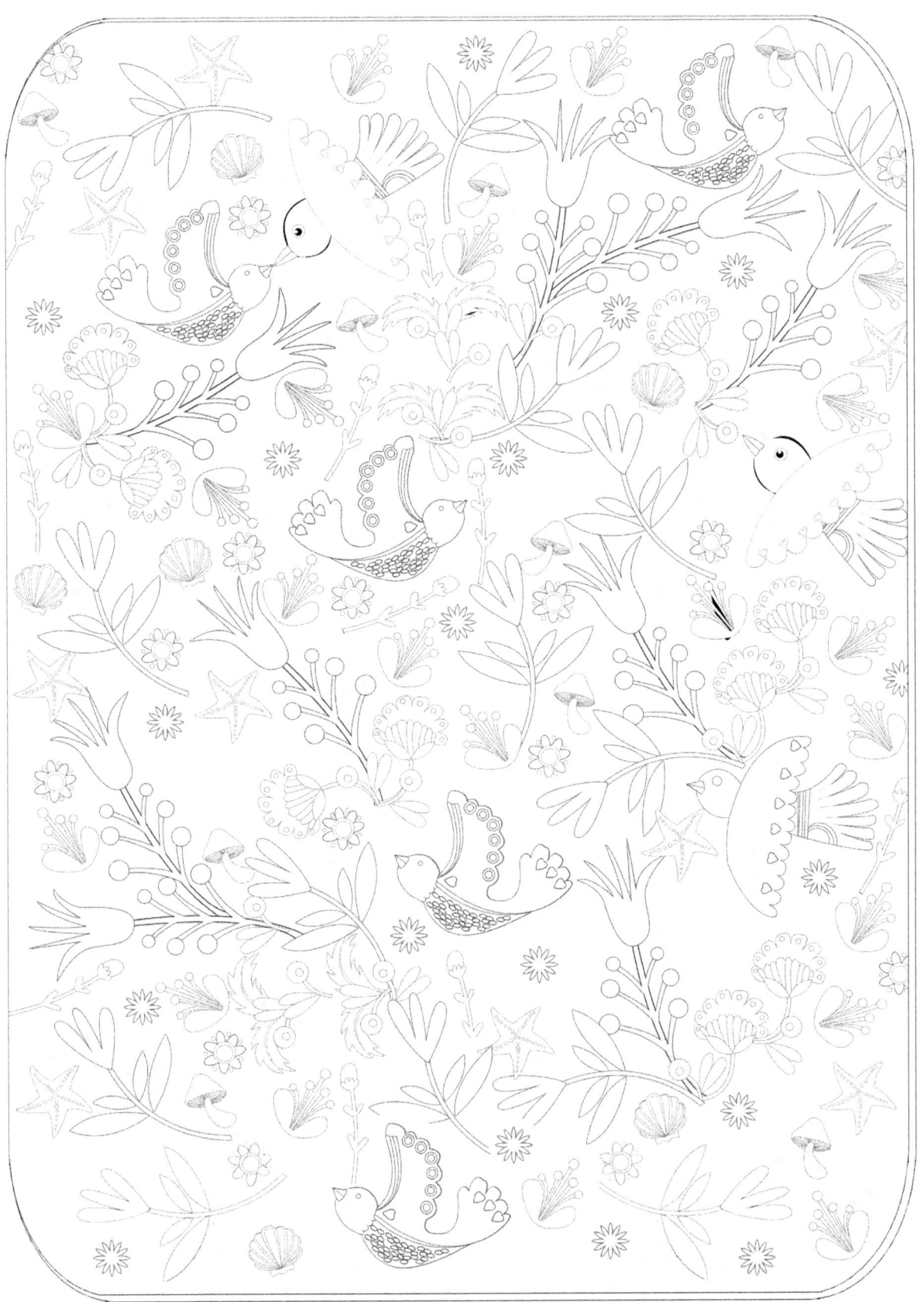

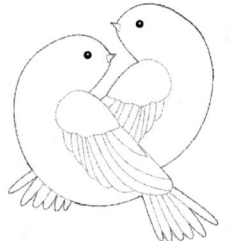

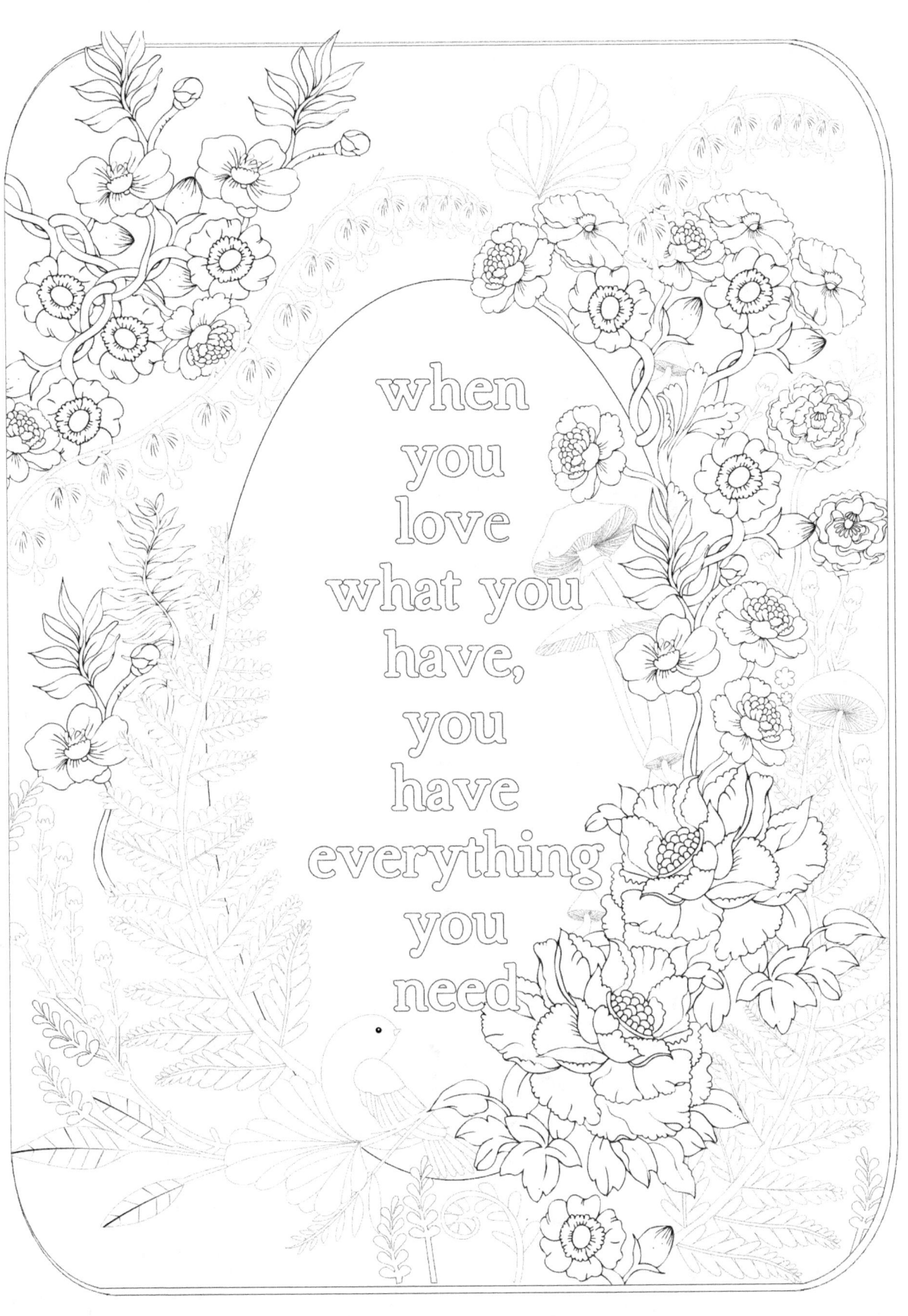

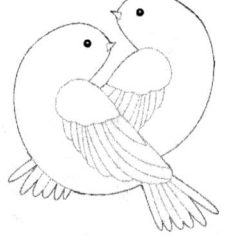

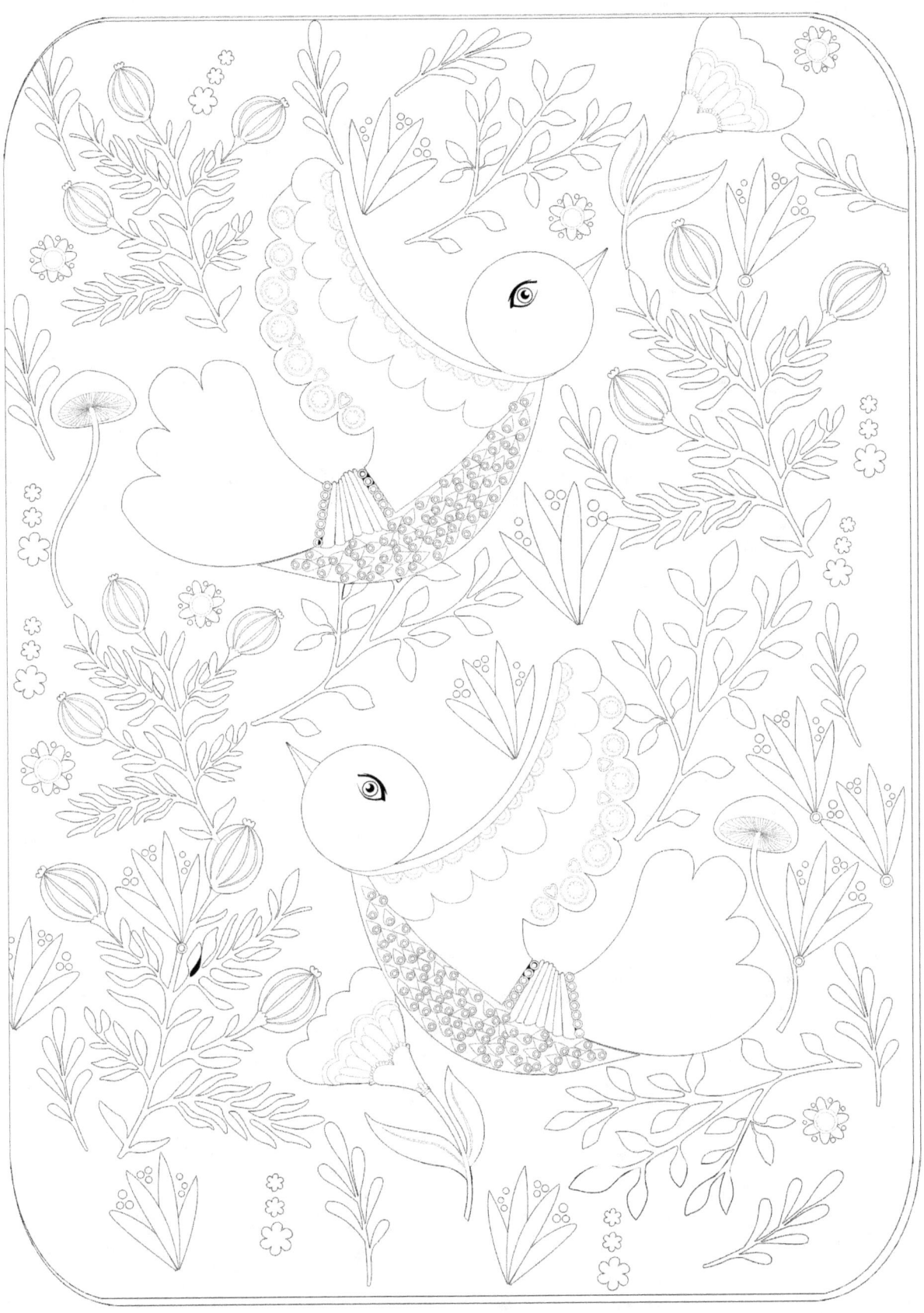

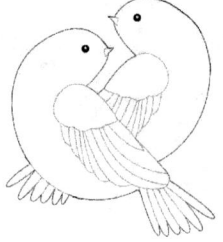

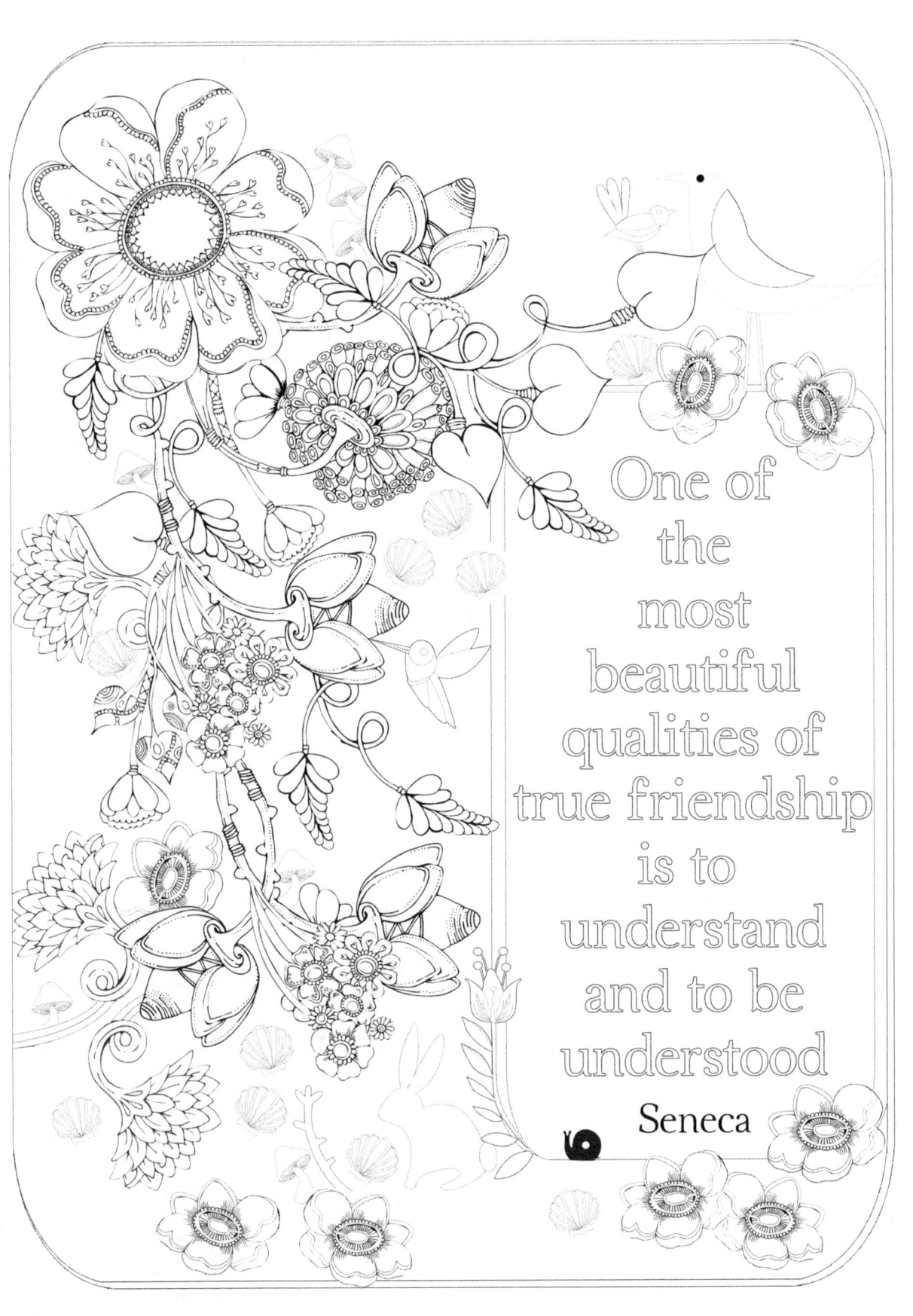

One of
the
most
beautiful
qualities of
true friendship
is to
understand
and to be
understood

Seneca

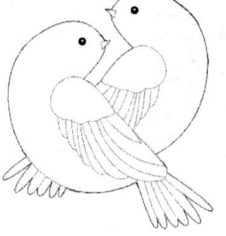

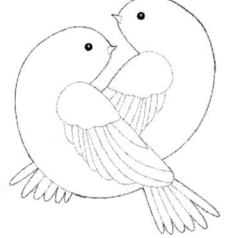

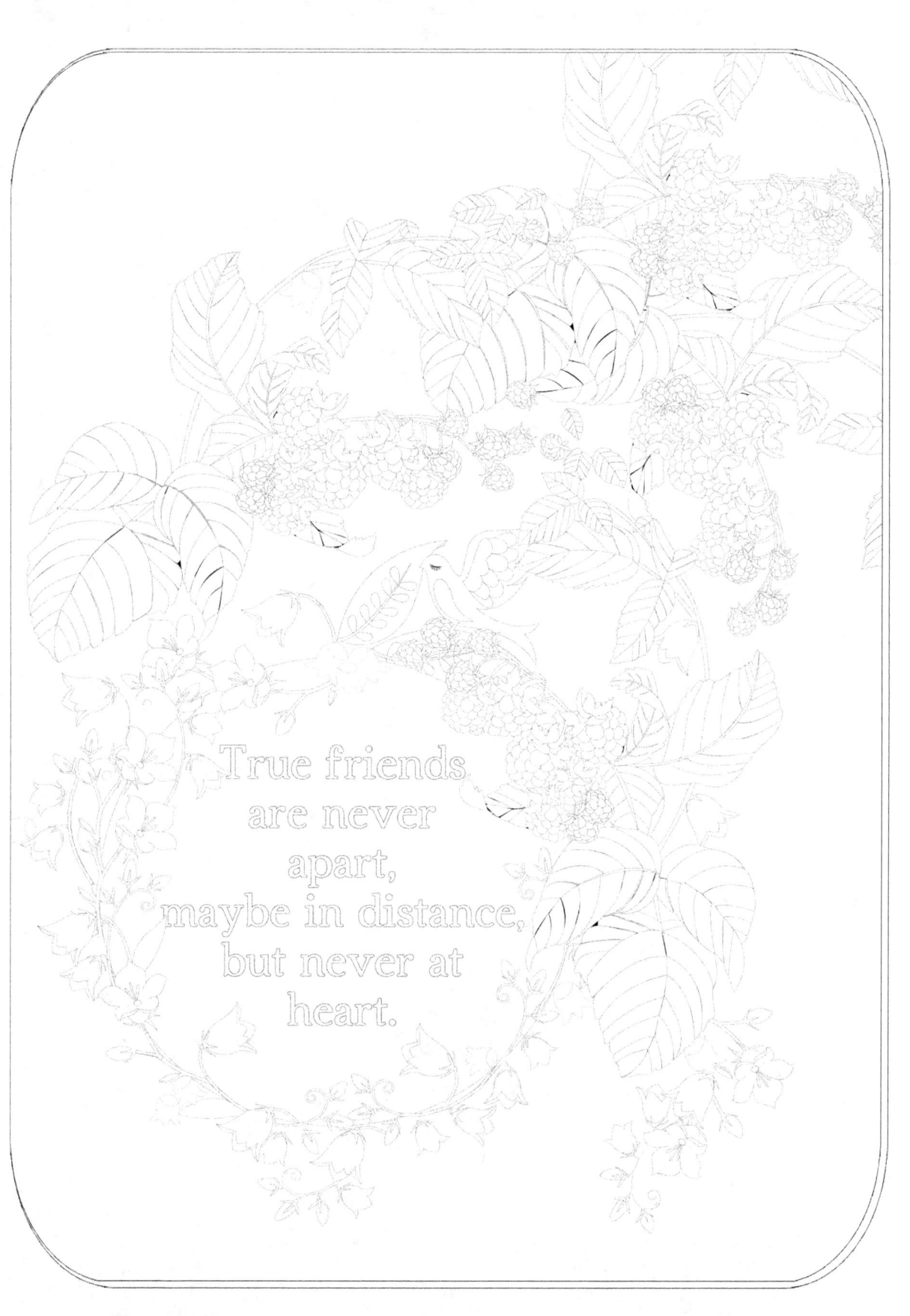

True friends
are never
apart,
maybe in distance,
but never at
heart.

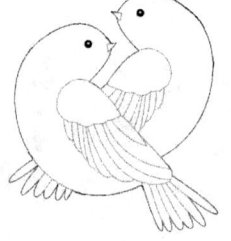

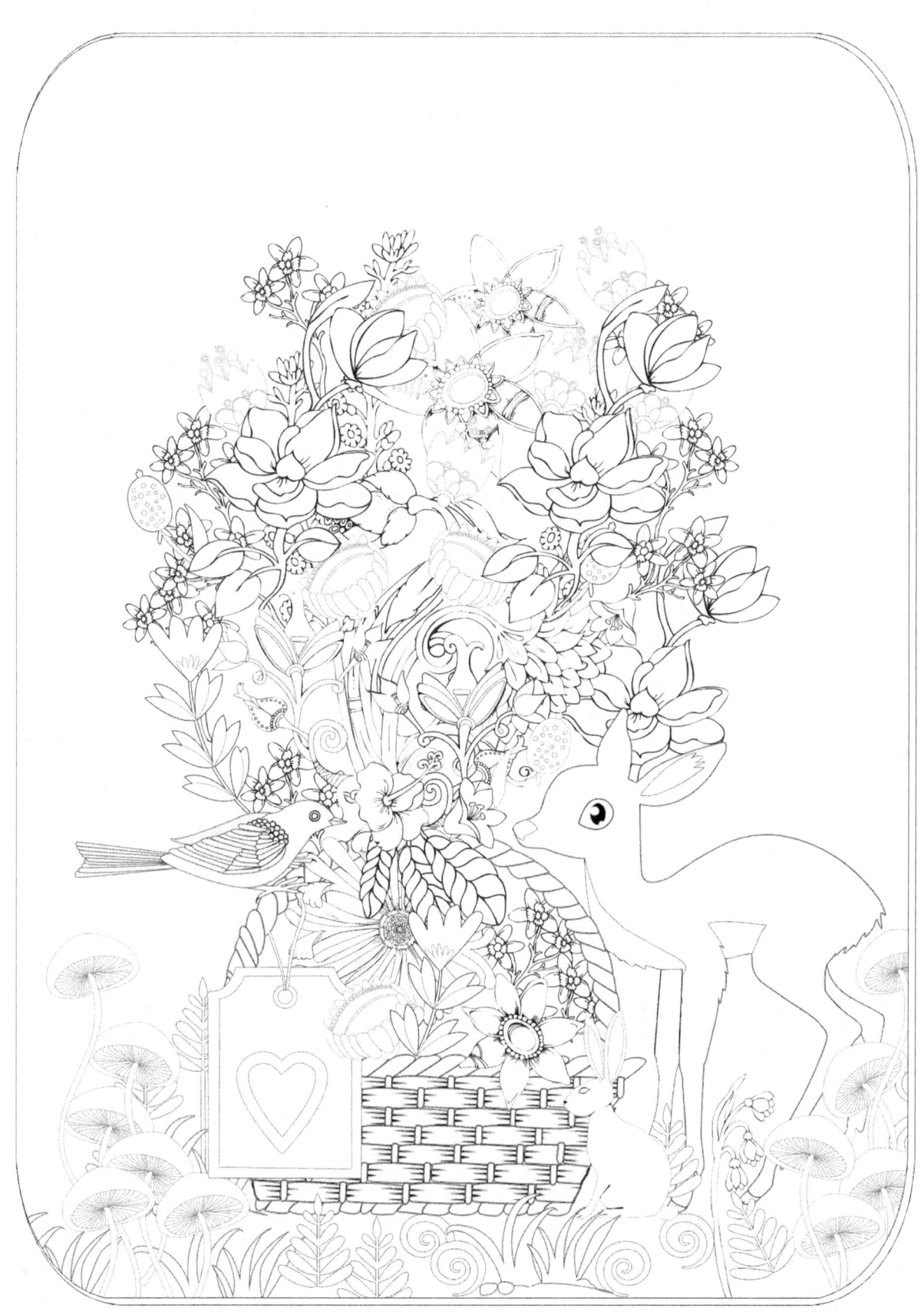

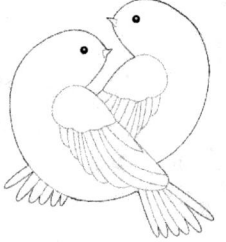

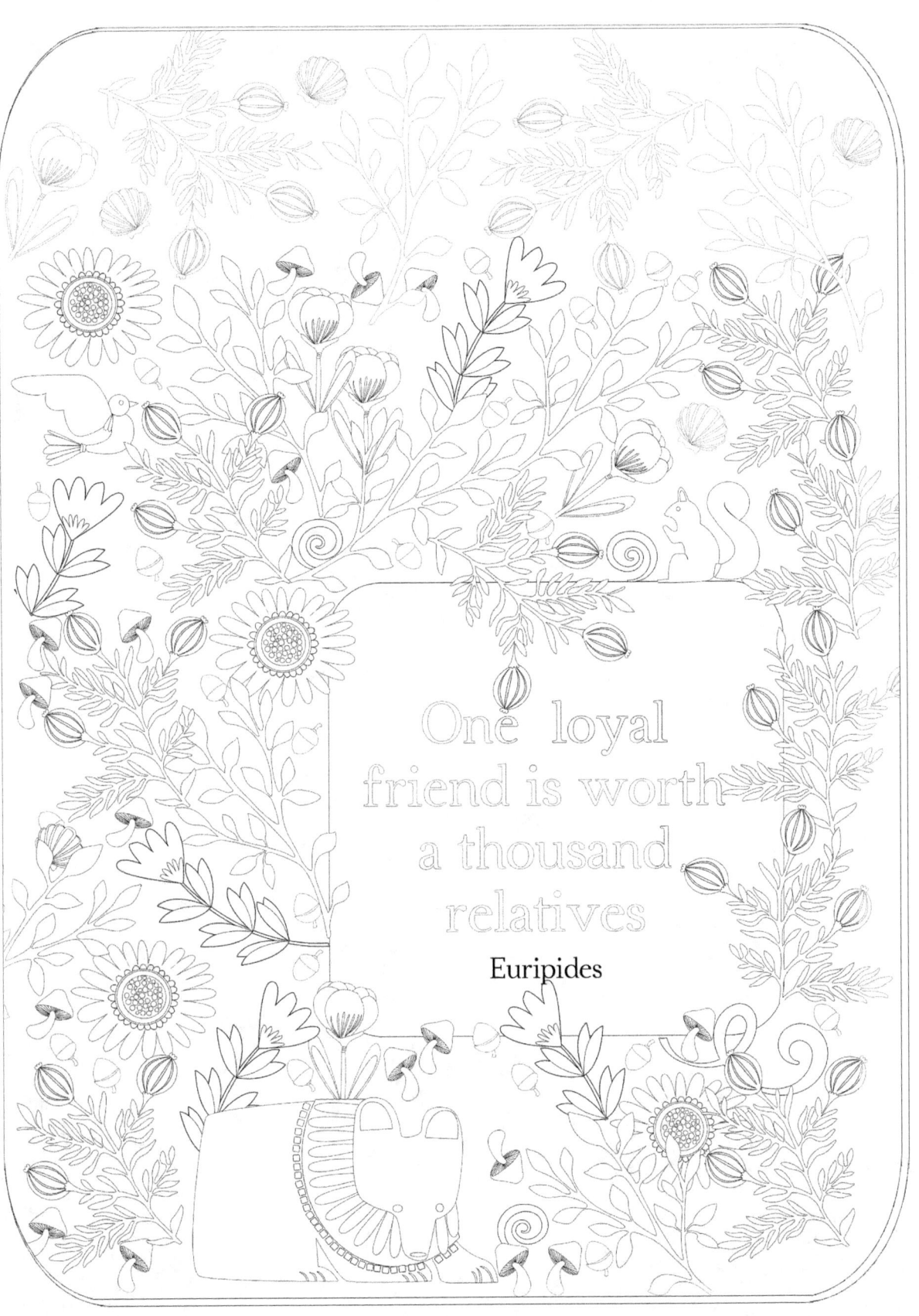

One loyal
friend is worth
a thousand
relatives

Euripides

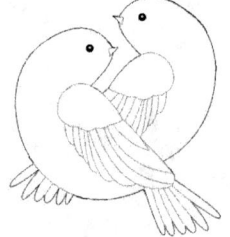

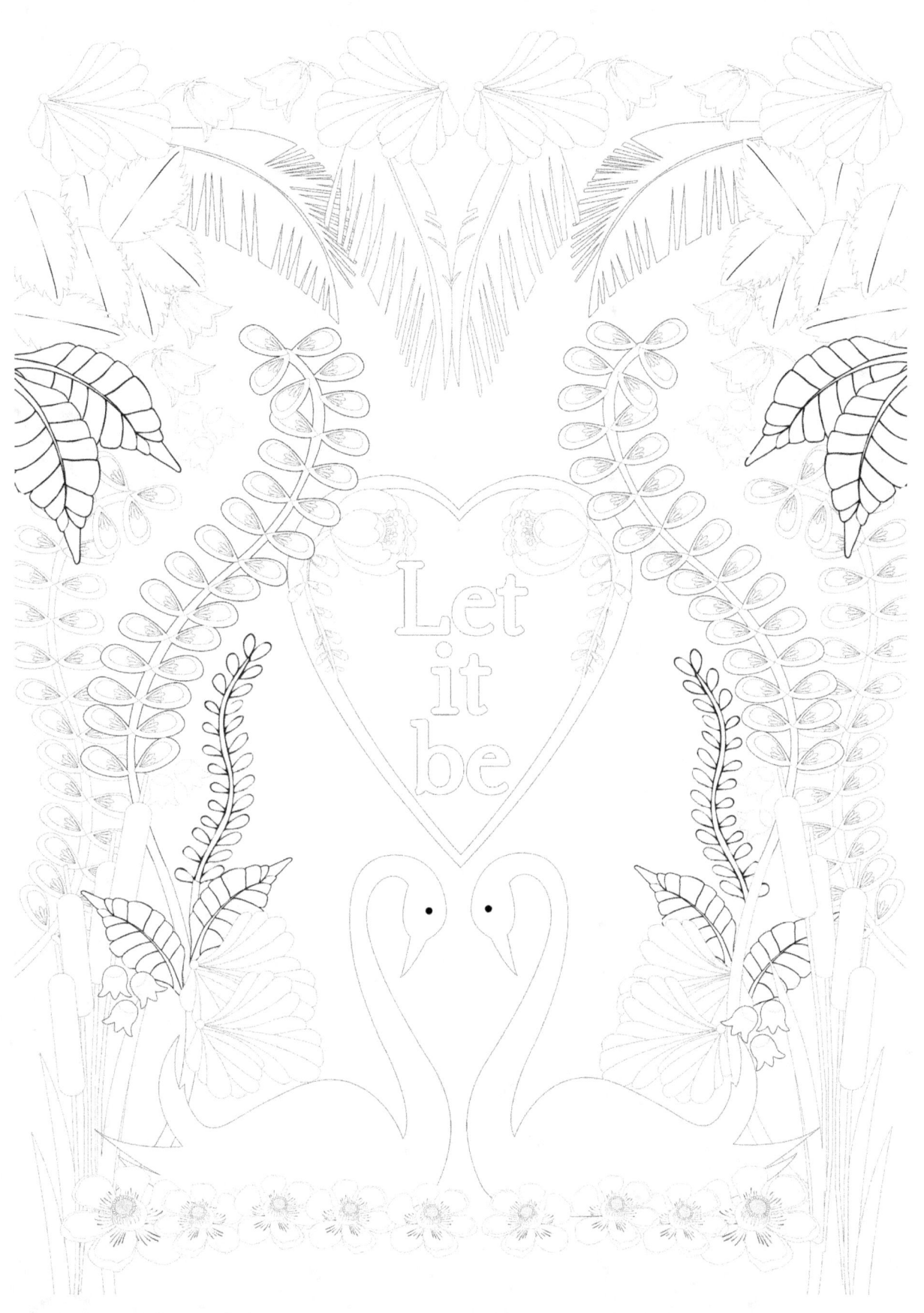

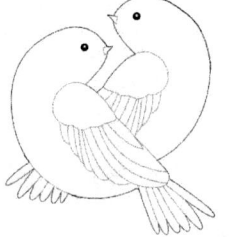

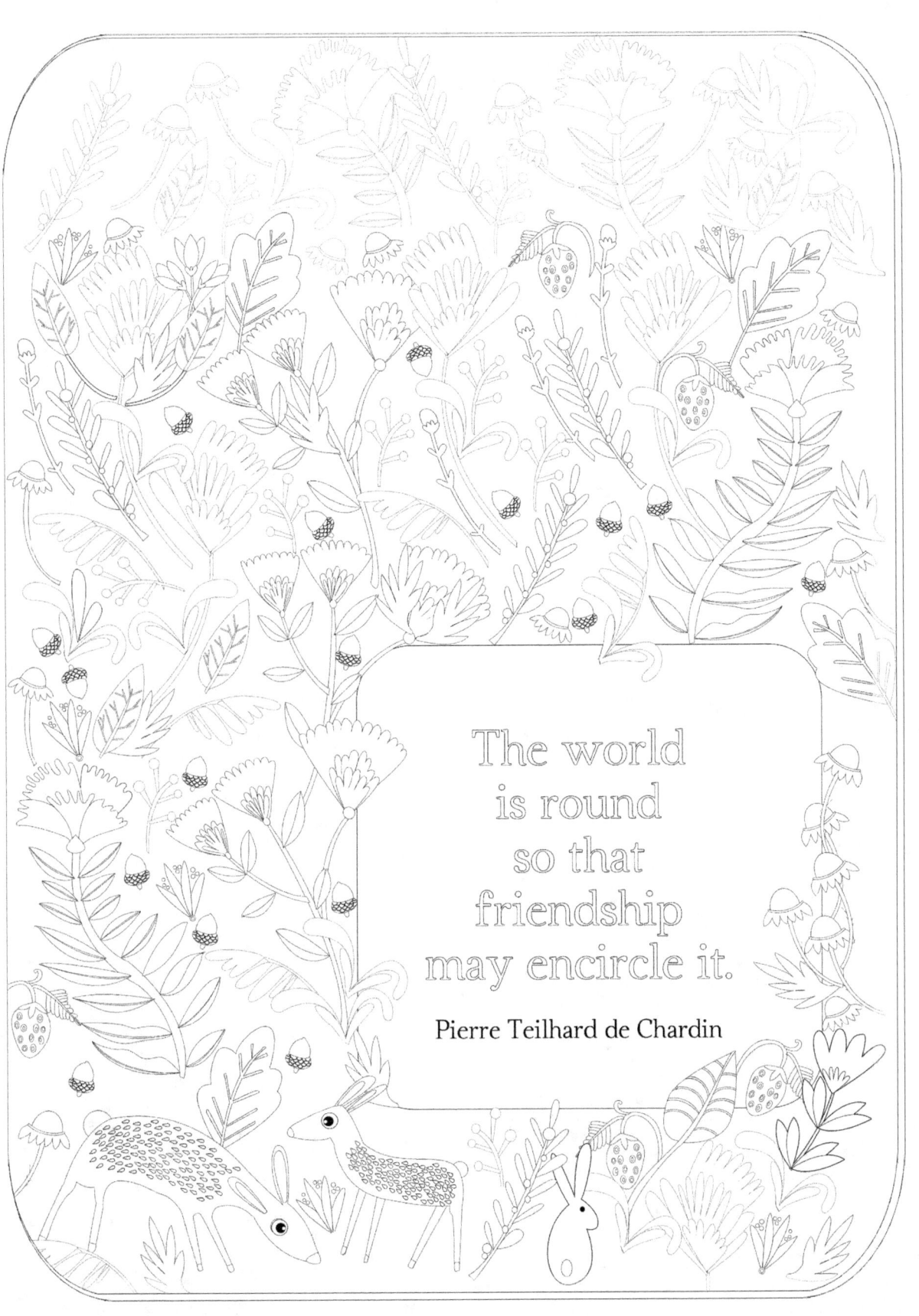

The world
is round
so that
friendship
may encircle it.

Pierre Teilhard de Chardin

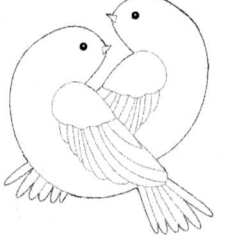

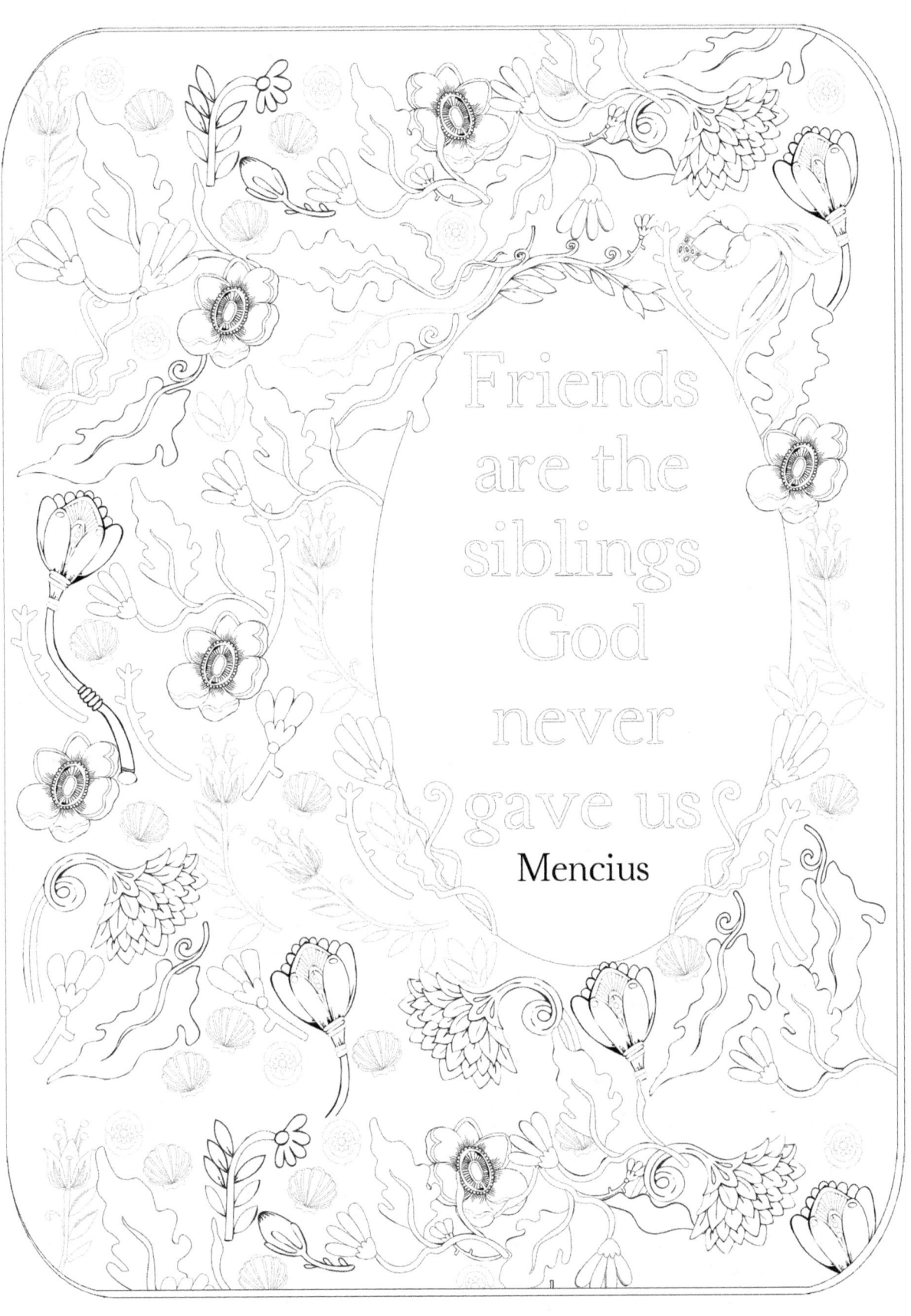

Friends
are the
siblings
God
never
gave us

Mencius

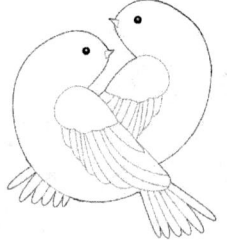

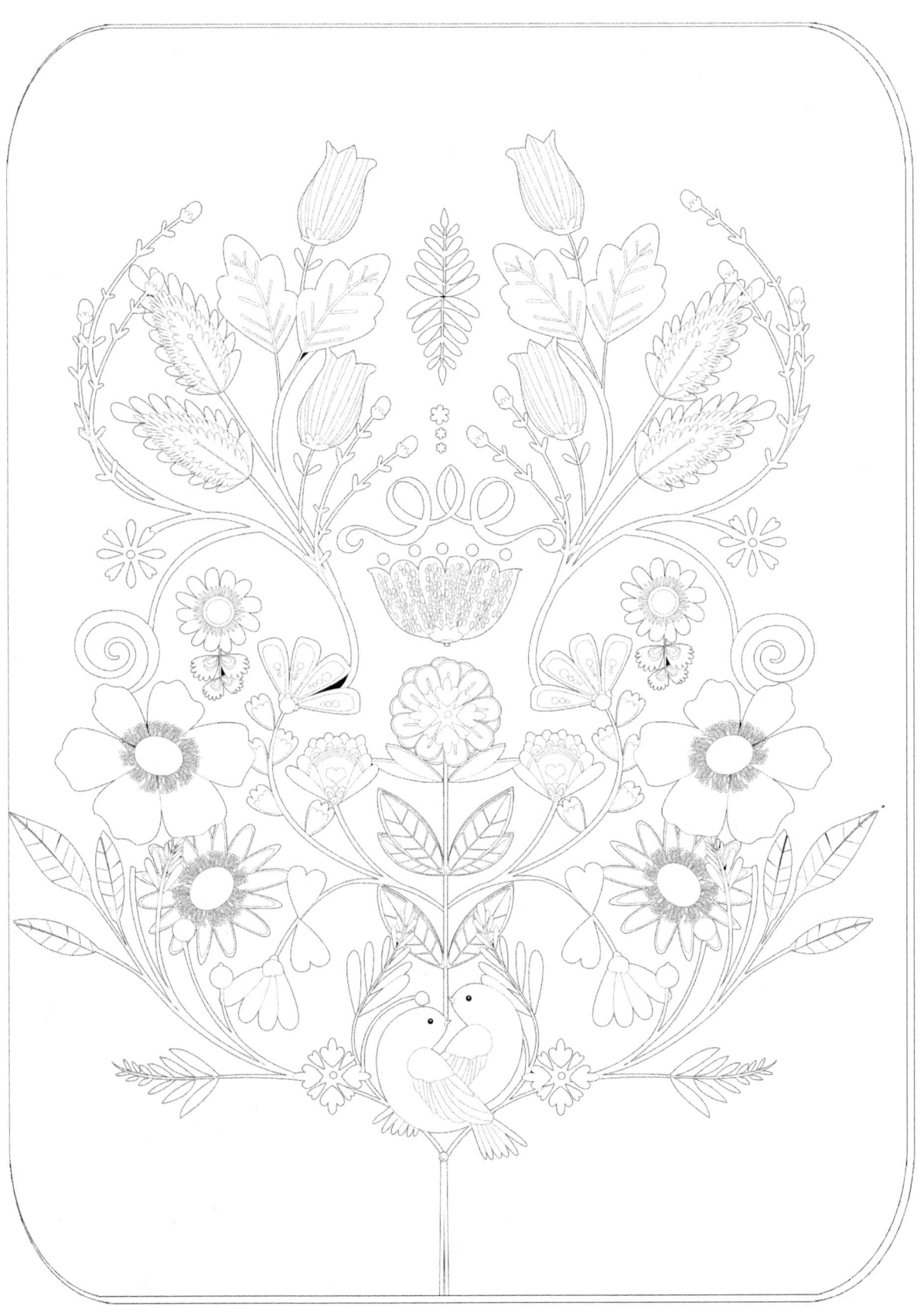

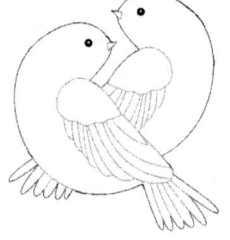

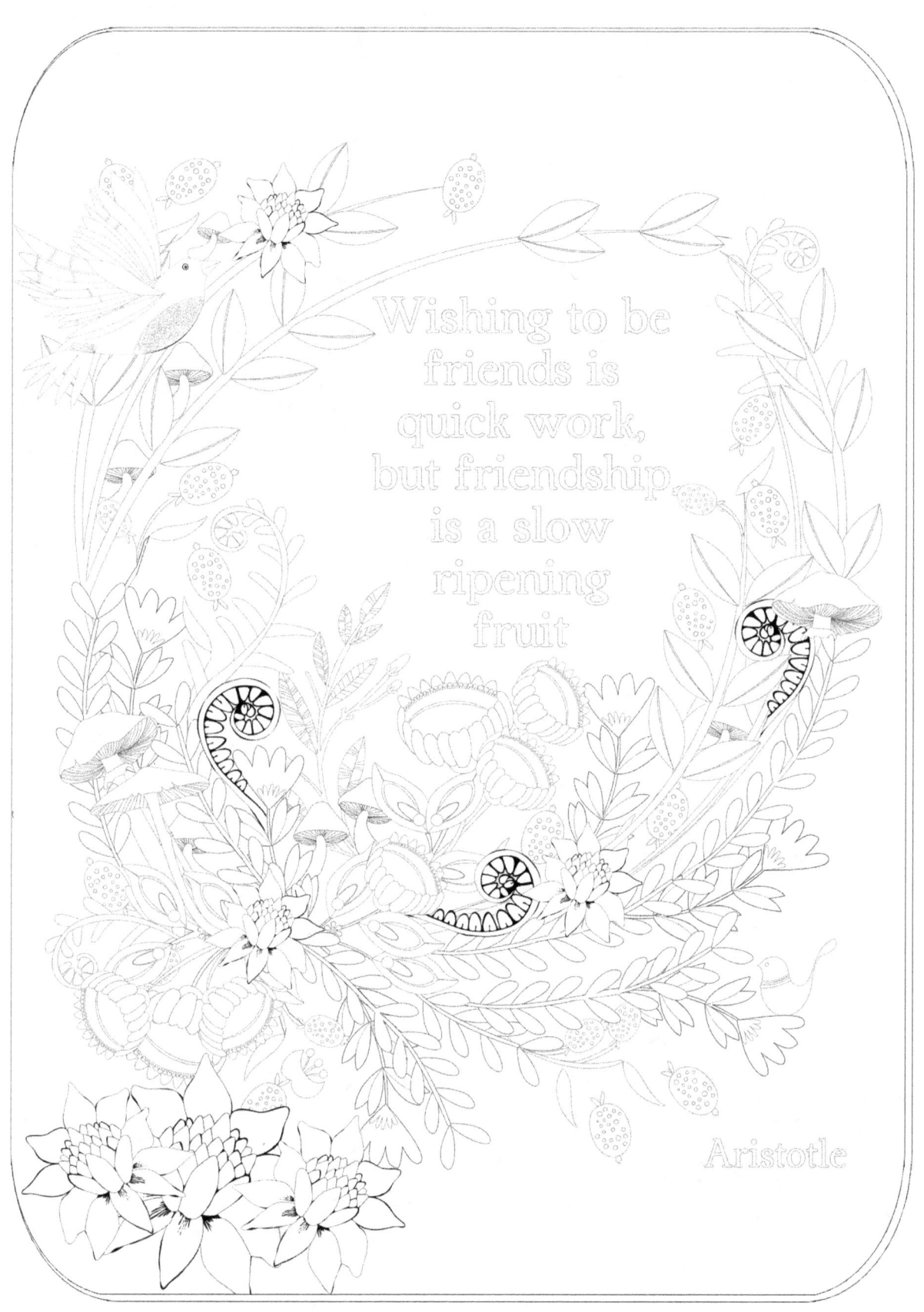

Wishing to be
friends is
quick work,
but friendship
is a slow
ripening
fruit

Aristotle

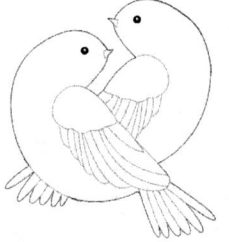

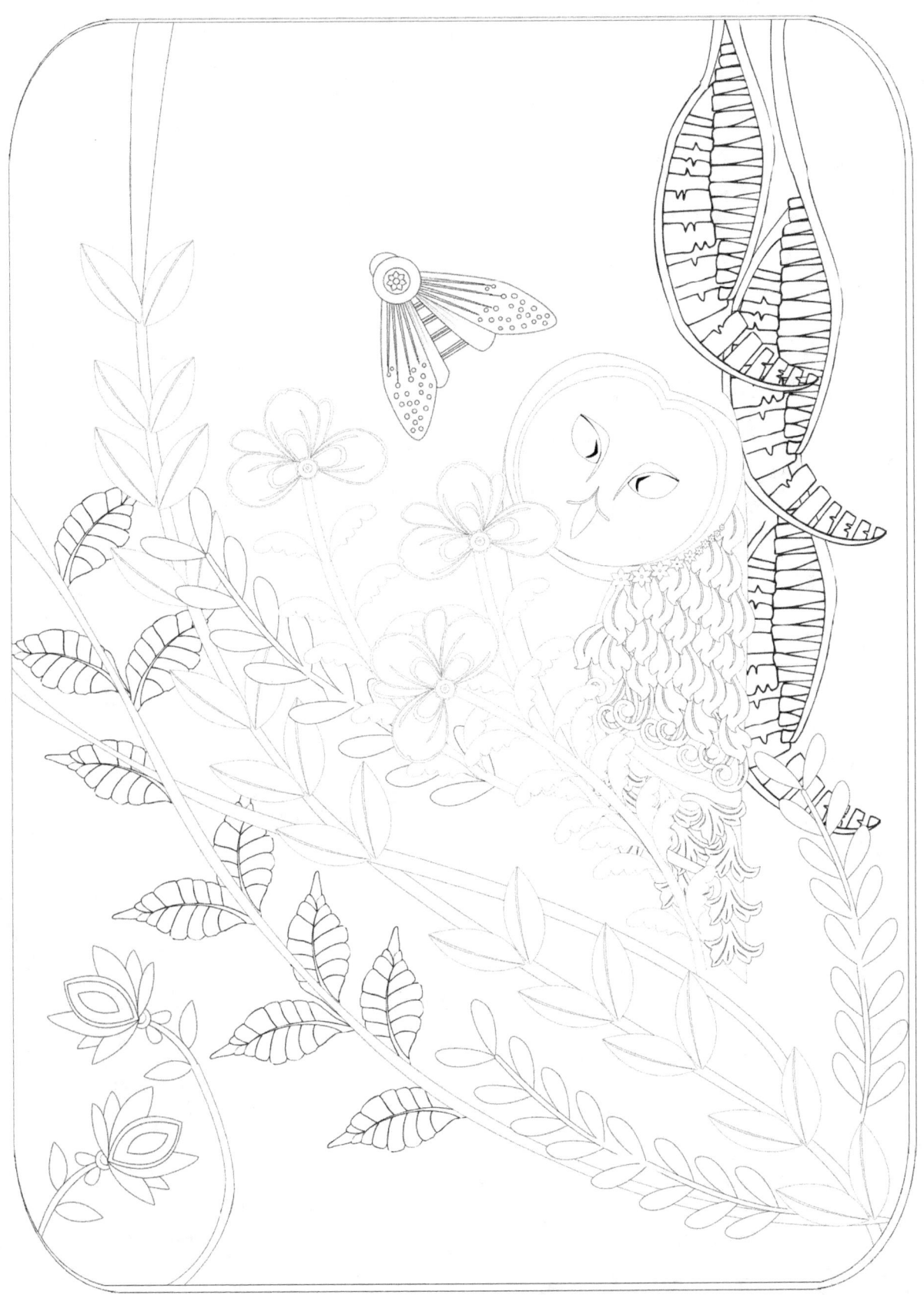

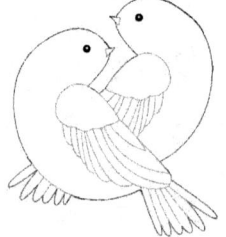

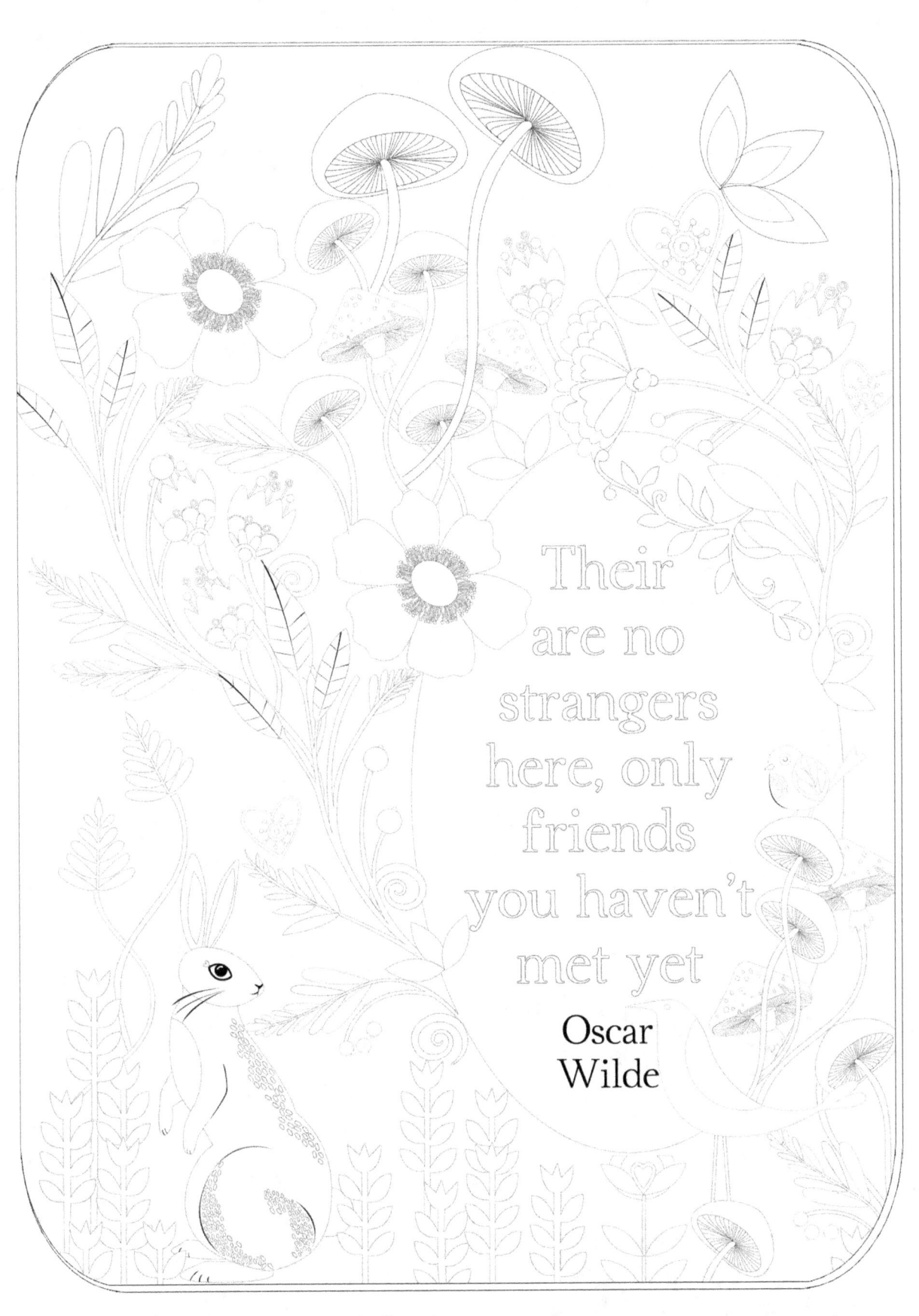

Their
are no
strangers
here, only
friends
you haven't
met yet

Oscar
Wilde

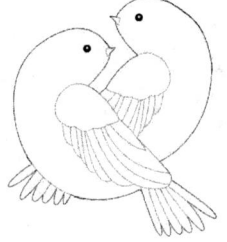

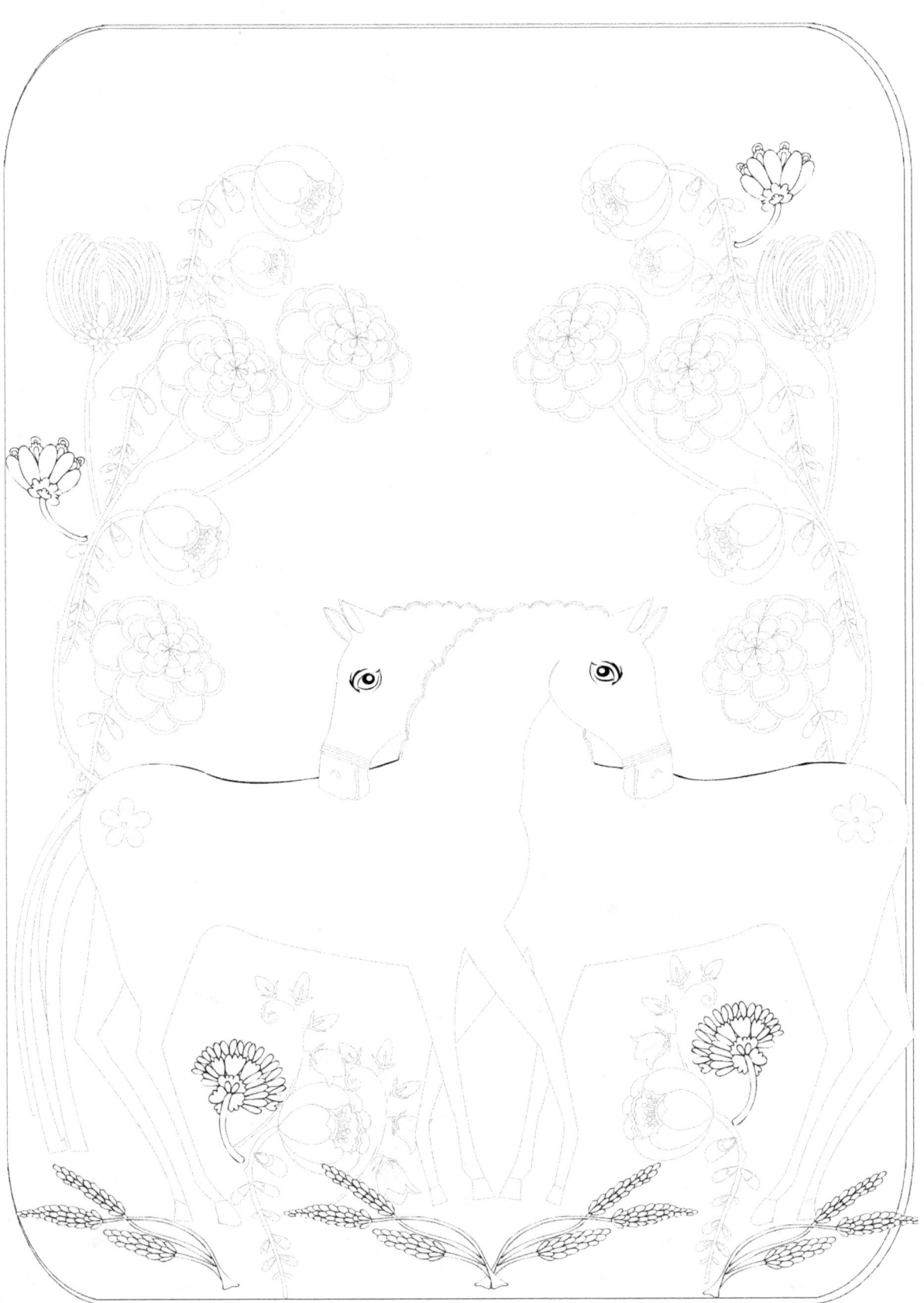

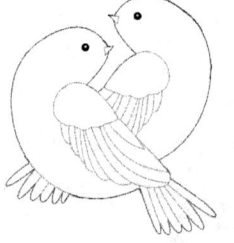

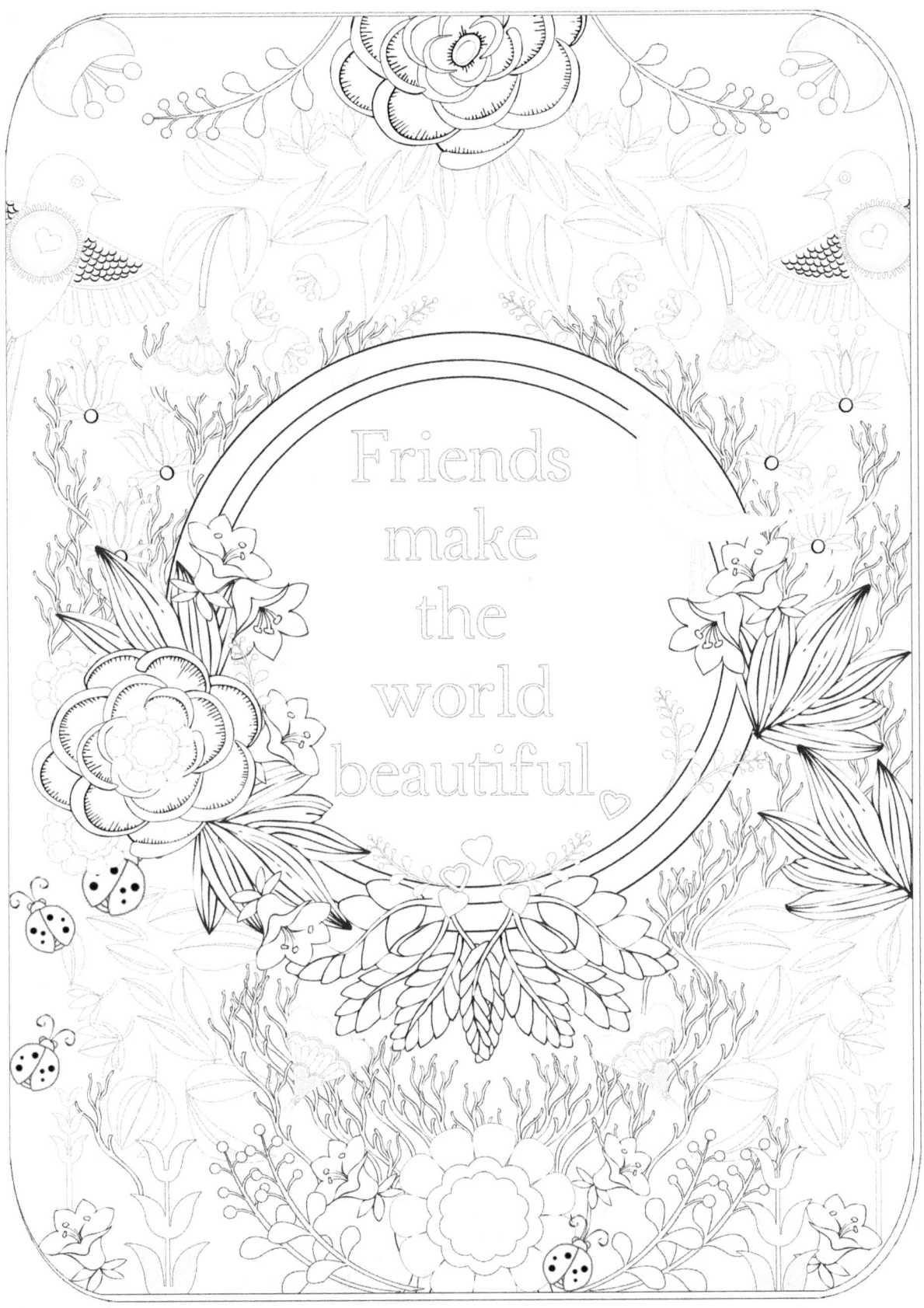

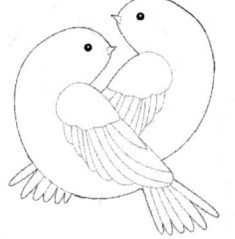

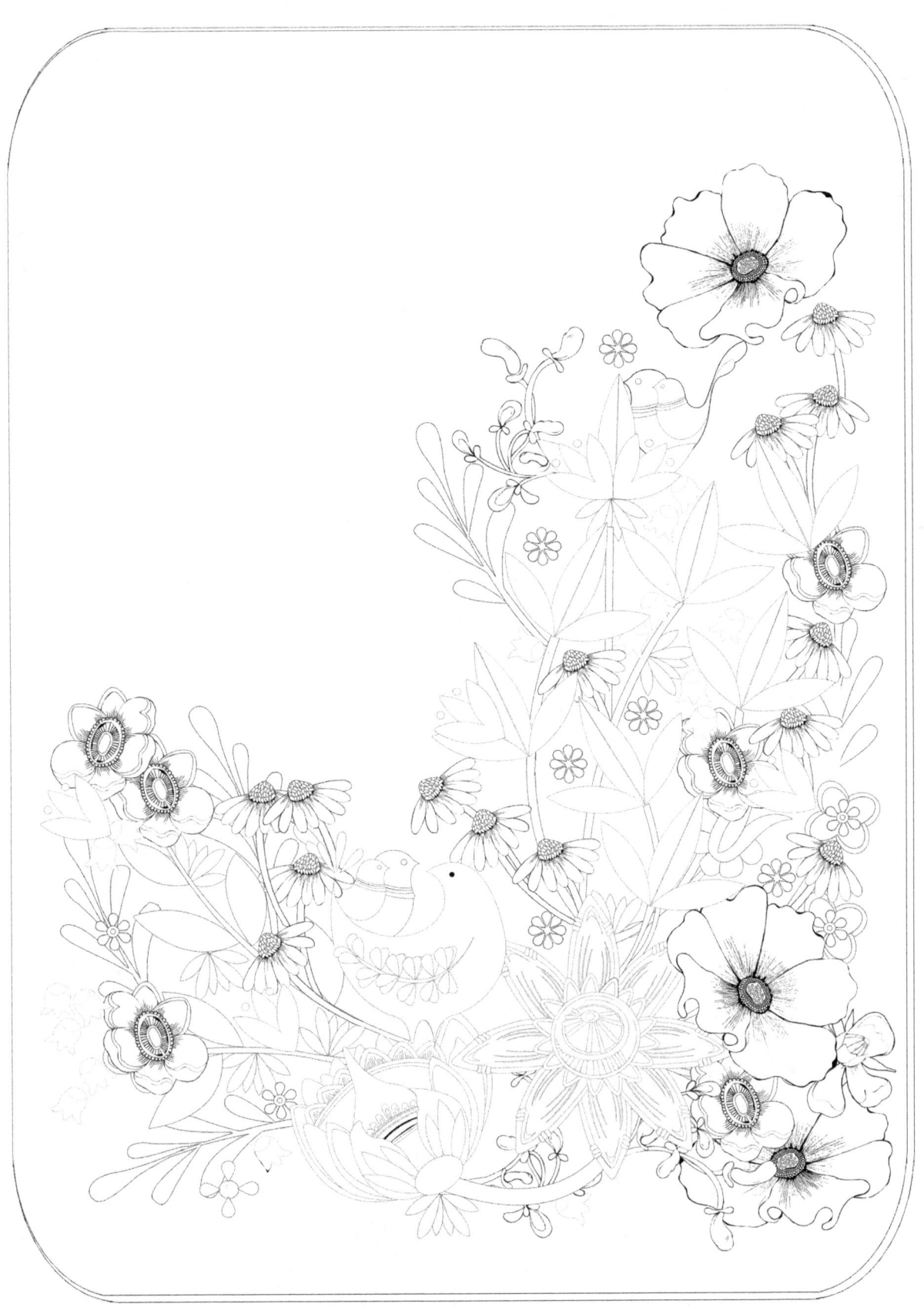

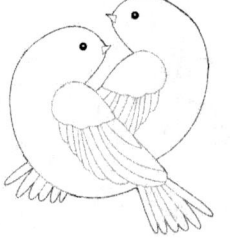

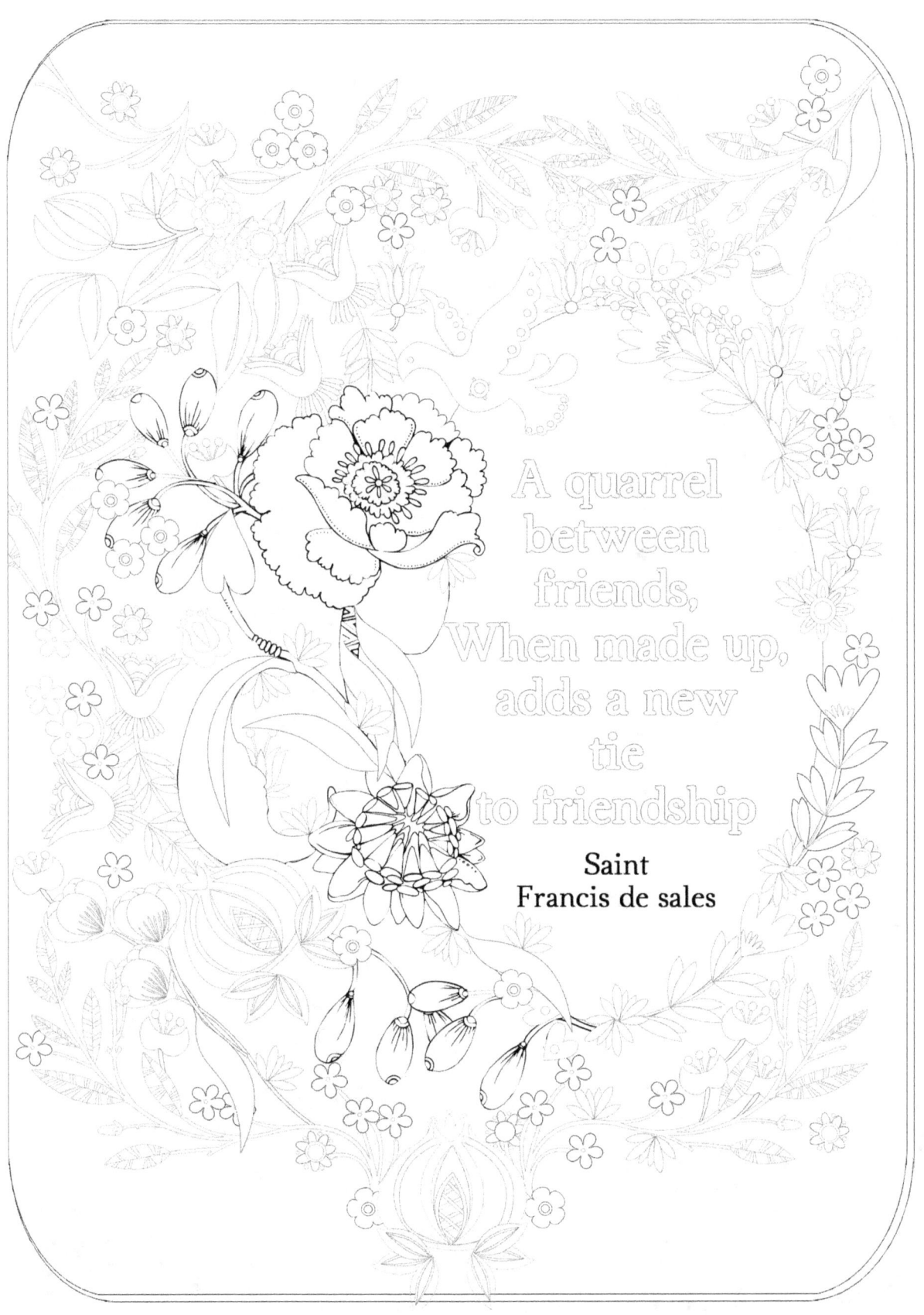

A quarrel
between
friends,
When made up,
adds a new
tie
to friendship

Saint
Francis de sales

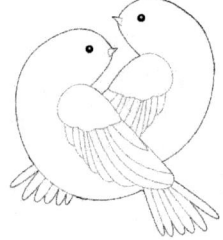

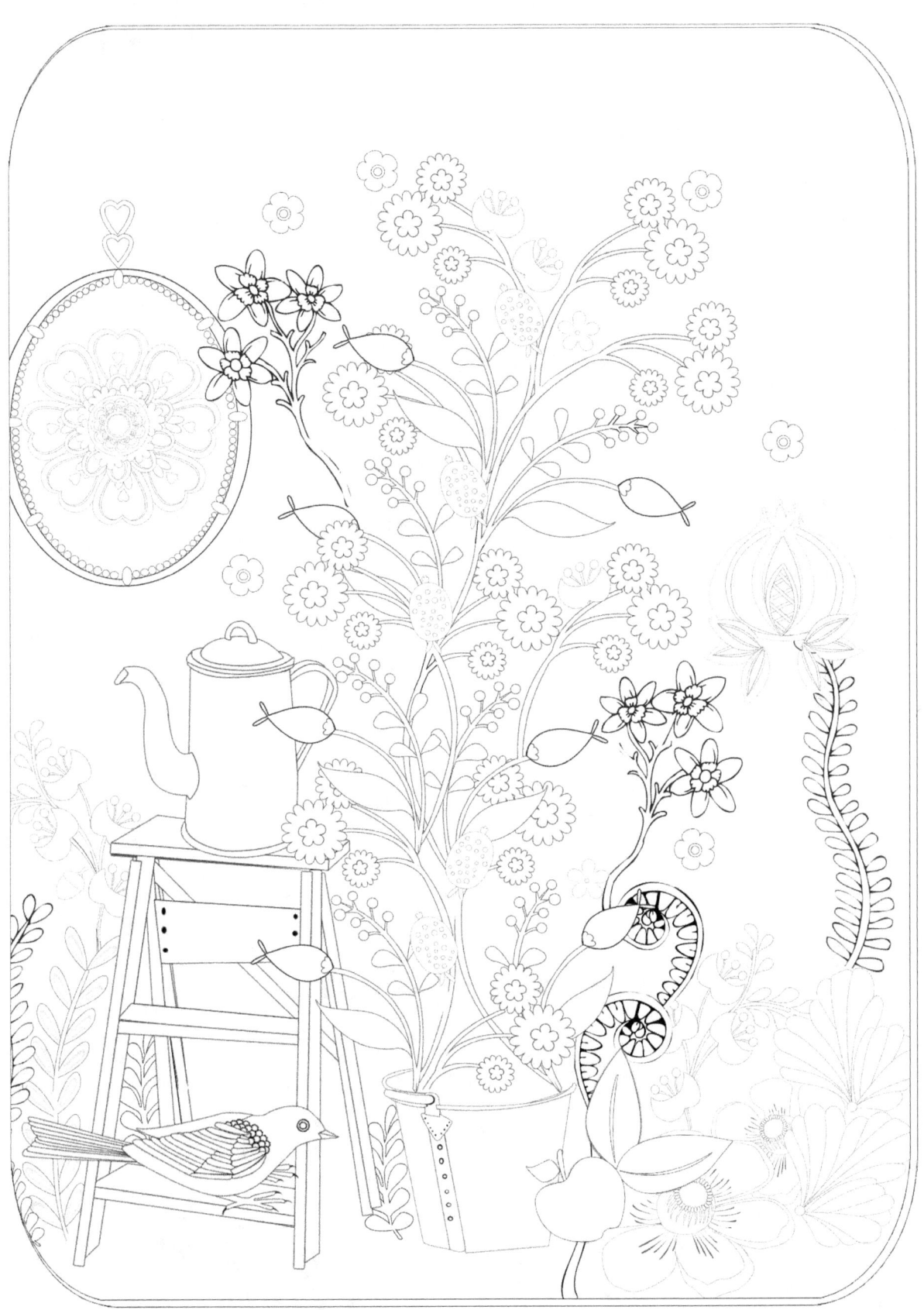

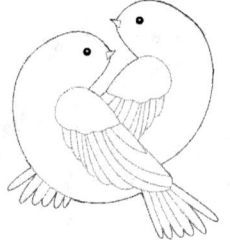

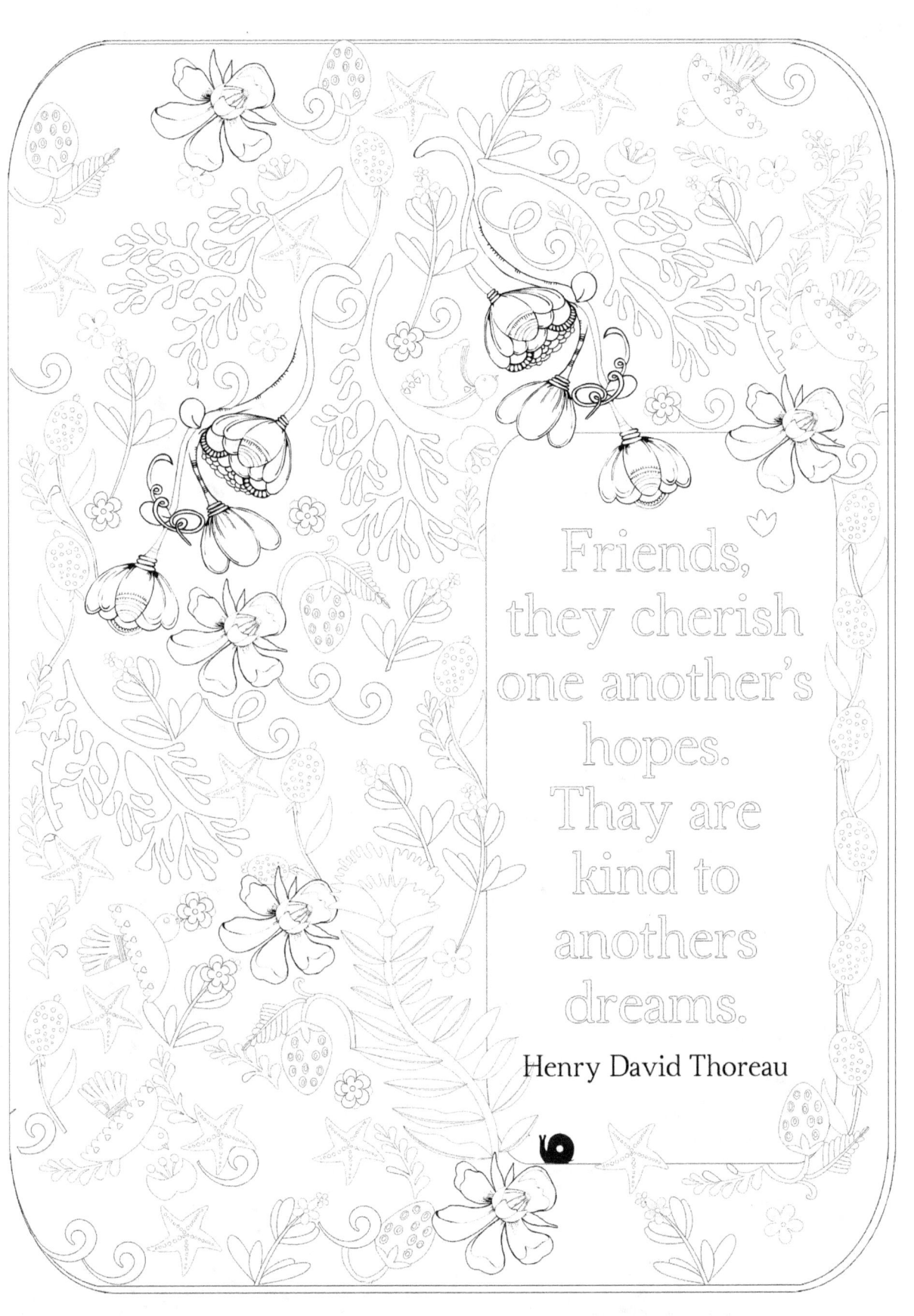

Friends,
they cherish
one another's
hopes.
Thay are
kind to
anothers
dreams.

Henry David Thoreau

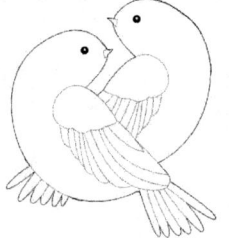

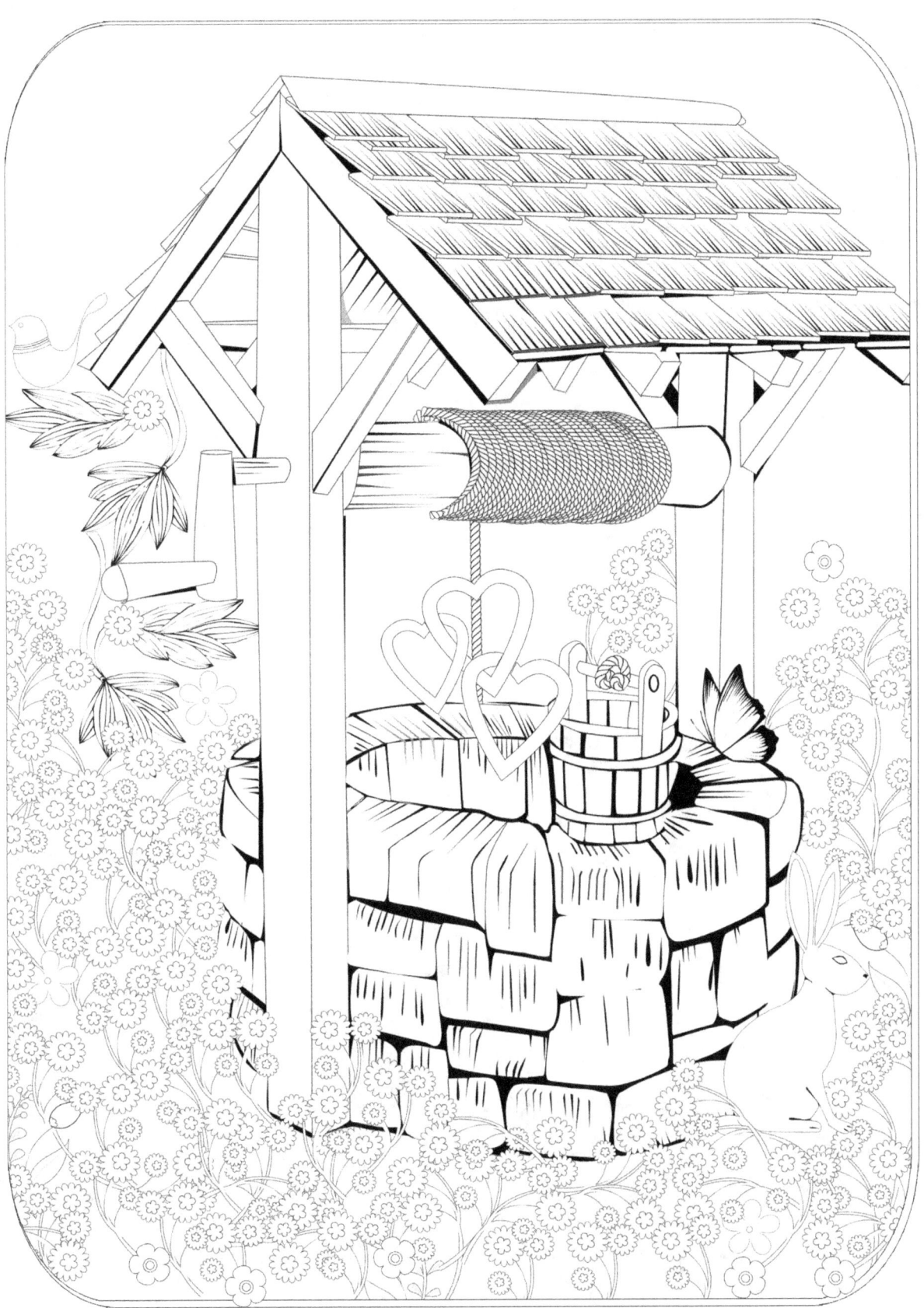

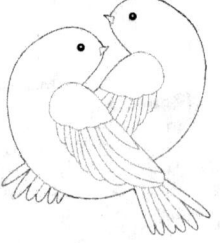

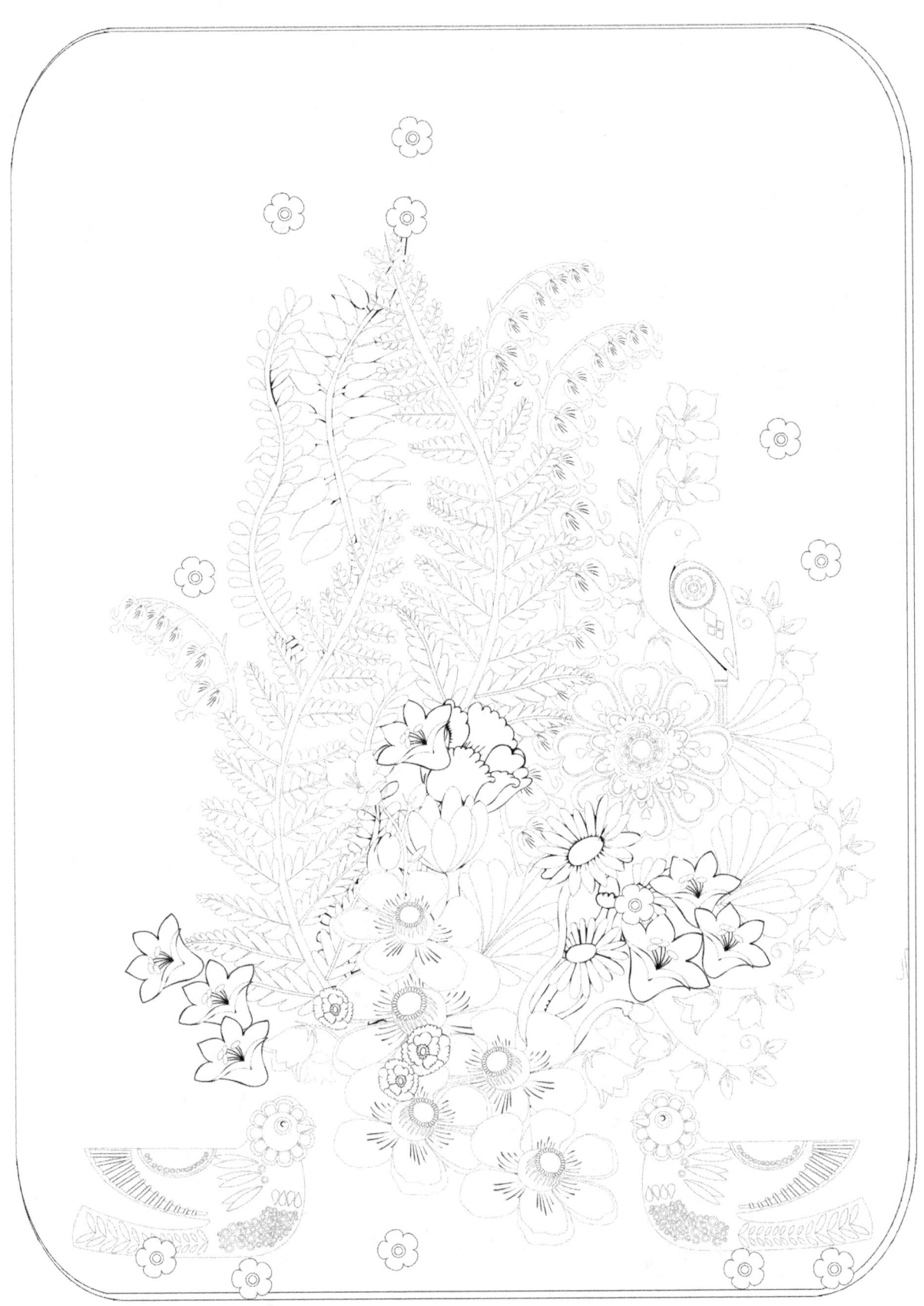

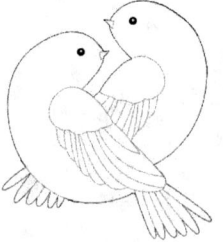

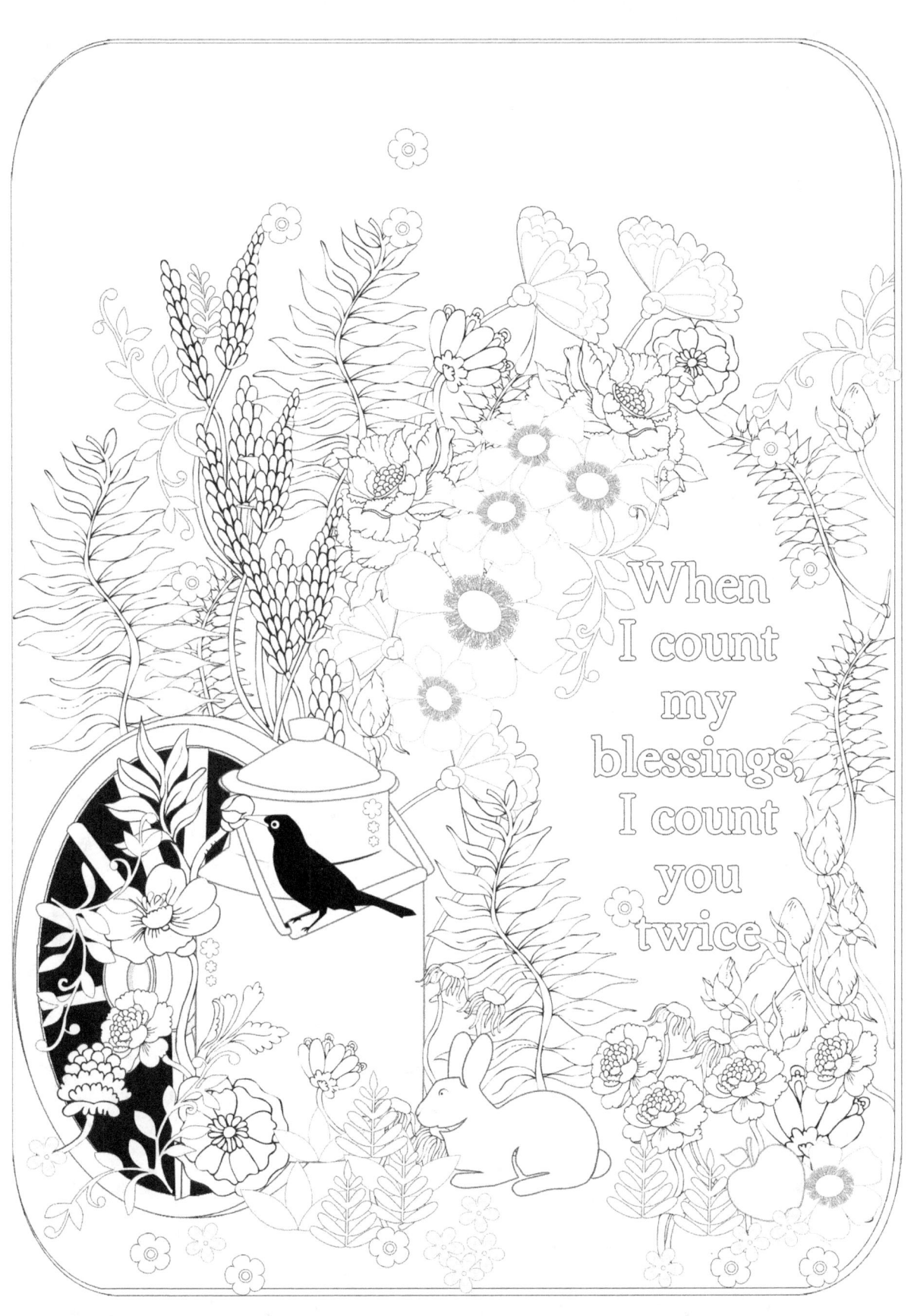

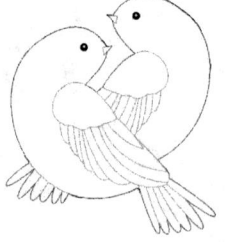

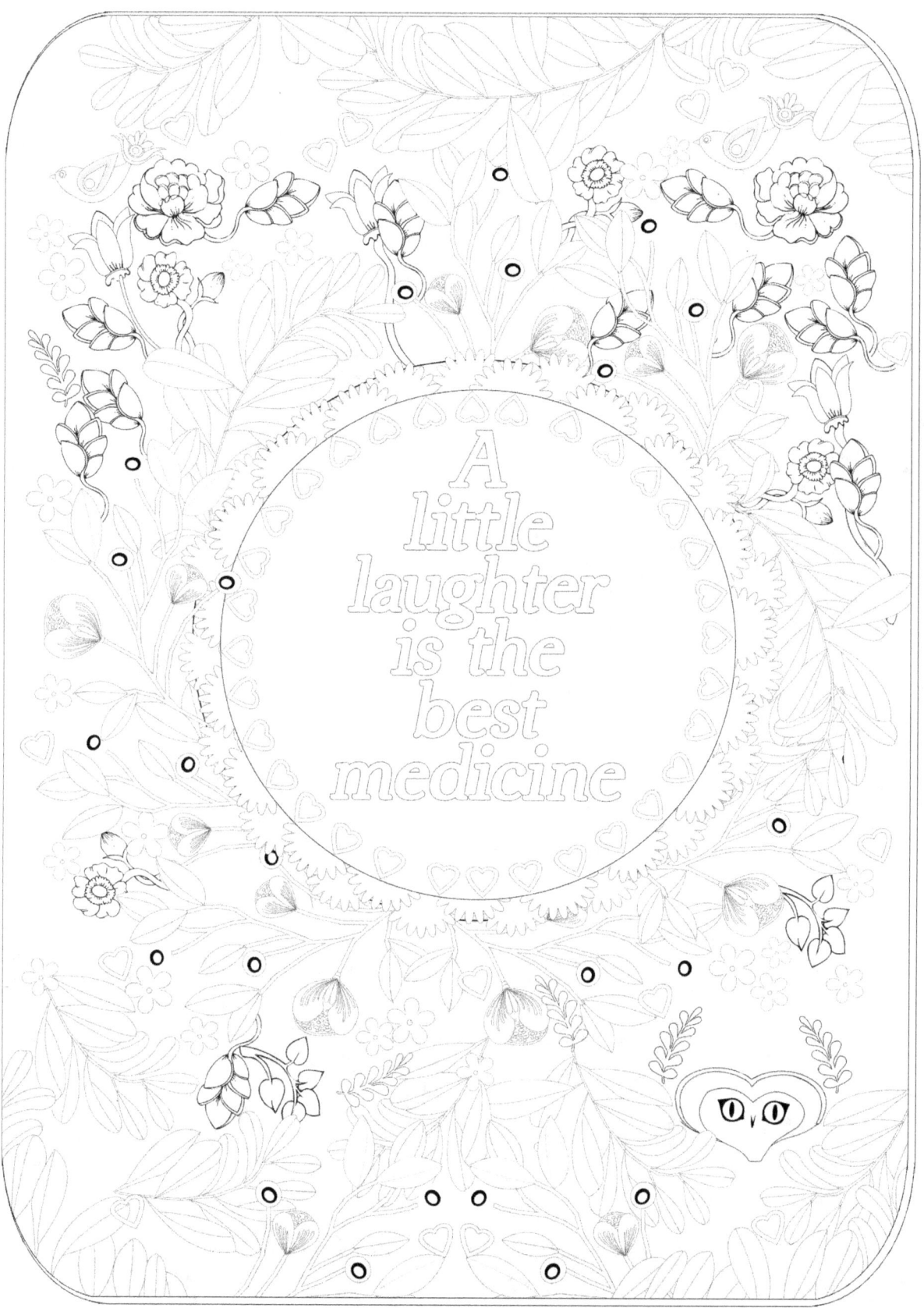

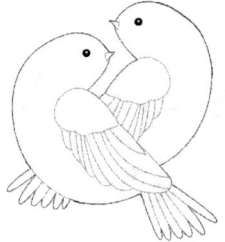

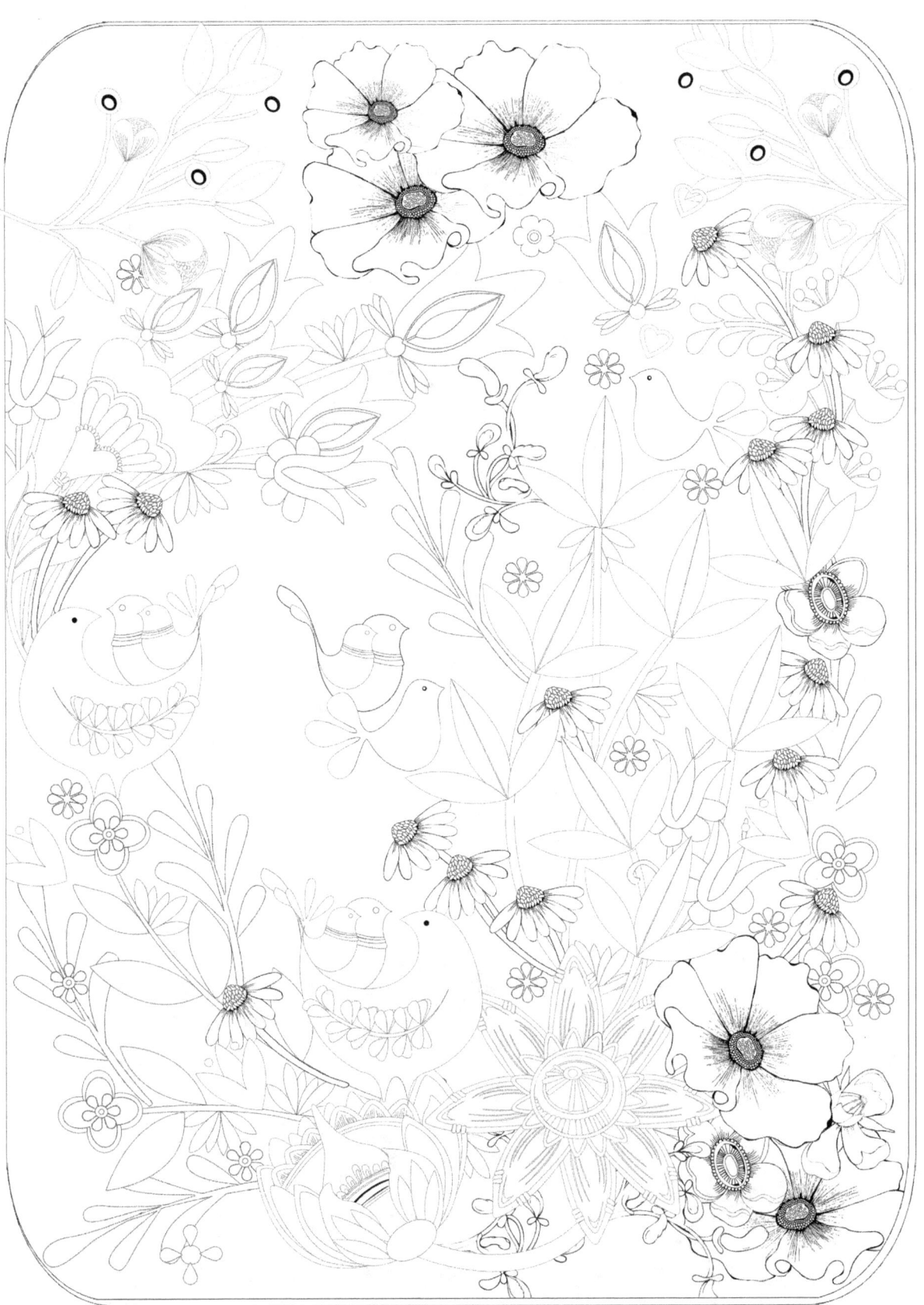

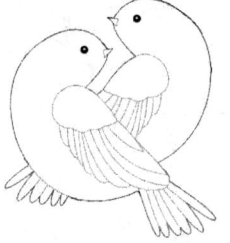

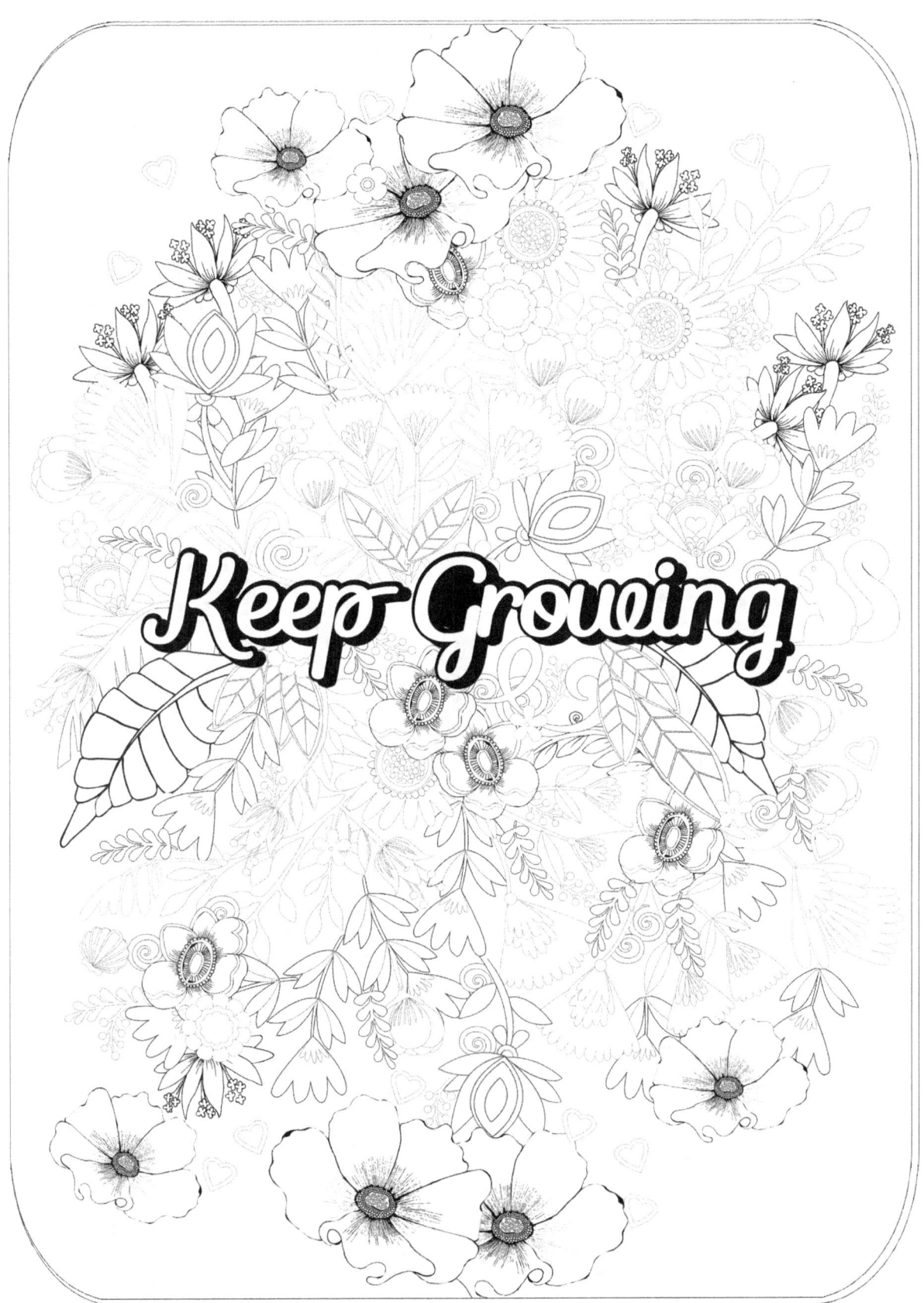

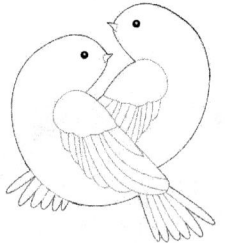

www.ingramcontent.com/pod-product-compliance
Lightning Source LLC
Chambersburg PA
CBHW081633220526
45468CB00009B/2418